BRIDGE BASICS 2

COMPETITIVE BIDDING

Audrey Grant

BARON BARCLAY

BRIDGE SUPPLY

Published by
Baron Barclay Bridge Supply

UPDATED EDITION

BRIDGE BASICS 2
COMPETITIVE BIDDING

Copyright © 2024 Audrey Grant's Better Bridge Corp.

Baron Barclay Bridge Supply
3600 Chamberlain Lane, Suite 206
Louisville, KY 40241
U.S. and Canada: 1-800-274-2221
Worldwide: 502-426-0410
Fax: 502-426-2044
www.BaronBarclay.com

Audrey Grant's Better Bridge
Toronto, ON Canada
1-888-266-4447
www.BetterBridge.com

ISBN 978-1-944201-38-8

FOURTEENTH PRINTING

Illustrations by Kelvin Smith
Design and composition by John Reinhardt Book Design

Printed in China

Contents

Introduction

Bridge Basics 2 Competitive Bidding, is important to keep your game current. Competitive bidding is popular. Players are more comfortable coming into the auction to prevent the opponents from easily reaching their best contract, to get to their own contract, and to suggest a lead.

In today's game, cuebids, preemptive jump overcalls, preemptive jump raises, and redoubles - to name a few calls - are used more than even a few years ago. Most of the tools used in competitive auctions are not considered conventions; they're now part of bridge basics.

After the opening bid, responder has guidelines. If you overcall, you are also opening the bidding for your partnership. Now, however, your partner isn't a responder; your partner is an advancer. The guidelines for responding and advancing aren't the same. It's important to know how to bid when the auction is competitive. This book gives you what you need to be comfortable whether playing face-to-face or online.

You can now play every one of the thirty-two Practice Deals from Bridge Basics 2 online with world-class robots. You're the declarer in each deal, sitting South. You can practice bidding, play, and defense, at your convenience. Scan the QR code, or download the Audrey Grant App and go to Practice Deals.

Thanks for being part of Better Bridge.

All the best,

Audrey Grant and the Better Bridge Team

1

Preemptive Opening Bids and the Subsequent Auction

Compare these two hands which, at first glance, seem to have little in common:

1)	♠ 6	2)	♠ K Q J 10 9 8
	♥ A K 7 4		♥ 5
	♦ A K 8 3		♦ 9 5 2
	♣ A 9 8 6		♣ 7 3 2

The first has 18 *high-card points* (*HCPs*) and the second only 6 high-card points. The first is within the 12-21 point range for an opening bid at the *one level*. The second doesn't have enough *strength* to open 1♠.

Yet these hands do have something in common. Both have five playing tricks – tricks you can expect to take if your partnership buys the *contract*. The first can be expected to take five tricks through the power of the *high cards*: the ♥A-K, ♦A-K, and ♣A. The second can take five tricks if spades are trumps, through the power of the long, strong spade suit.

Since both can take five tricks, it seems clear both should qualify for an opening bid. However, although the first hand meets the requirements for an opening bid at the one level, the second does not since a 1♠ opening bid would describe a hand with about 12-21 points. To take advantage when there is a good, long suit but less than the values for an opening bid, the classic *preemptive opening bid* was introduced.

Requirements for Preemptive Opening Bids

Preemptive bids need a place on the *Bidding Ladder* for opener to show a hand strong in playing tricks but not in high-card strength. The general idea is you have a good suit but not enough strength to open at the one level.

- A six-card suit is opened at the *two level*.
- A seven-card suit is opened at the three level.
- An eight-card suit is opened at the four level.

A good suit is typically headed by two of the top three *honors* or three of the top five honors. For example:

- ♥A-Q-8-6-5-2. This suit has two of the top three honors, the ♥A and ♥Q.
- ♠K-J-10-7-5-4-2. This suit has three of the top five honors, the ♠K, ♠J, and ♠10.
- ♦K-10-8-5-4-2 would not be considered a good six-card suit since it has only two of the top five honors, the ♦K and ♦10.

Preemptive opening bids are popular in today's game because they have a number of advantages:

- They interfere with the opponents' *auction*.
- They describe the hand to partner.
- They suggest an *opening lead* to partner if the partnership ends up defending.

There are risks in making a preemptive bid. An opening 3♠ bid, for example, could make it challenging for *responder* to bid effectively when holding a good hand. A lot of bidding room has been taken up. Also, having overbid, opener may be *defeated* in the 3♠ contract and lose points to the opponents.

In general, however, the advantages tend to outweigh the disadvantages, which is why preemptive opening bids are popular.

For example, consider South's dilemma with this hand if East opens 3♠:

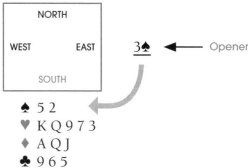

♠ 5 2
♥ K Q 9 7 3
♦ A Q J
♣ 9 6 5

With 12 high-card points plus 1 *length point* for the five-card heart suit, South was planning to open the bidding 1♥. After East opens 3♠, South is faced with a challenge. To bid hearts, South would have to start at the four level and bid 4♥. That might get the partnership much too high. If South passes, however, the partnership might miss the best contract. East's preemptive opening bid has made it more likely North-South might bid too much or too little.

West has a well-defined description of East's hand: a good seven-card spade suit and less than the values for an opening bid at the one level. West can use this information to decide How High to compete for the contract. If South does become *declarer* and West is on opening lead, West can lead a spade expecting East to have values in the spade suit.

It's for these reasons preemptive bids are an integral part of *competitive bidding*.

Preemptive Opening Bids on the Bidding Ladder

The preemptive opening bids are shaded on the *Bidding Ladder*. At the two level, they are referred to as *weak two-bids*. Notice they only apply to opening bids of 2♦, 2♥, and 2♠. The opening bid of 2♣ is reserved for very strong hands of about 22 or more points – too strong to open at the one level.

	OPENING BID	POINTS	DESCRIPTION
		OPENING BIDS AT A HIGHER LEVEL ARE RARE	
GAME 29+ PTS.	5♦	Not enough for an opening bid at the one level	Good 9-card or longer suit
	5♣		About 8 playing tricks
	4NT		
GAME 26+ PTS.	4♠	Not enough for an opening bid at the one level	Good 8-card or longer suit
	4♥		
	4♦		About 7 playing tricks
	4♣		
GAME 25+ PTS.	3NT		Partnership Agreement
	3♠	Not enough for an opening bid at the one level	Good 7-card suit
	3♥		
	3♦		About 6 playing tricks
	3♣		
	2NT	20-21	Balanced
	2♠	Not enough for an opening bid at the one level	Good 6-card suit
	2♥		
	2♦		About 5 playing tricks
	2♣	22+	Strong, artificial; any shape
	1NT	15-17	Balanced
	1♠		5+ spades
	1♥	12-21	5+ hearts
	1♦		3+ diamonds
	1♣		3+ clubs

Hands Meeting Requirements for a Preemptive Opening

♠ 7
♥ K Q J 10 9 8
♦ 10 7 3
♣ 9 6 2

2♥. This is an ideal hand for a weak two-bid opening. There are only 6 high-card points plus 2 length points, not enough to open 1♥. The solid heart suit will produce five playing tricks with hearts as the trump suit.

♠ 8 6
♥ Q 5 2
♦ Q J 10 8 7 3
♣ 7 6

2♦. This hand barely qualifies for a weak two-bid. There are only 5 high-card points, putting this on the low end of the scale. The suit does have three of the top five honors, but you wouldn't want to have much less. Missing the ♦A and ♦K, you could expect only four playing tricks.

♠ 6
♥ A Q J 9 8 7 4
♦ 8 3
♣ 9 4 2

3♥. With only 7 high-card points plus 3 length points for the seven-card suit, there is not enough strength to open 1♥. However, 3♥ describes the hand well and will make the auction more challenging for the opponents if they have the majority of the strength.

♠ K Q 9 8 6 5 4 2
♥ 8
♦ J 10 3
♣ 4

4♠. With only 6 high-card points plus 4 length points for the eight-card spade suit, there is not enough strength to open 1♠. A preemptive opening bid of 4♠ describes the hand and will make it difficult for the opponents to reach their best contract.

Hands Not Meeting Requirements for a Preemptive Opening

♠ 10 8 6 5 4 3
♥ A 10 3
♦ 8 6
♣ K J

Pass. The suit quality isn't good enough for a weak two-bid although there is a six-card suit. With only 8 high-card points, you would pass. There is no guarantee of taking more than two or three tricks with spades as the trump suit.

♠ 4 2
♥ K 7 2
♦ A K J 9 7 3
♣ J 8

1♦. There is a good six-card suit and enough strength to make an opening bid at the one level, 12 high-card points plus 2 length points for the six-card suit. This is the priority.

♠ J 8 7 6 4 3 2
♥ K 10 5
♦ A 7
♣ 6

Pass. The quality of the seven-card suit isn't good enough for a three-level opening bid. There is no guarantee of taking more than three or four tricks with spades as the trump suit. This hand illustrates the importance of having a good suit for a preemptive opening. With only 8 high-card points plus 3 length points, there isn't enough strength to open at the one level.

♠ 8 7 5
♥ J 6 3
♦ 3
♣ A Q J 10 5 4

Pass (3♣). Although there is a strong six-card club suit, you can't open a weak two-bid in clubs. The 2♣ opening is reserved for other purposes. Probably best to pass, although some might open 3♣, treating the good six-card suit as a seven-card suit.

Raising Opener's Preemptive Bid

Since opener is showing a long suit and suggesting it as trumps, responder will generally want to play with opener's suit as trumps. When planning on raising opener's suit, there are two considerations:

- If there are likely enough combined tricks for *game*, responder can *raise* to the game level.

- If there are not enough tricks for game, responder can further the preempt by raising to the level corresponding to the number of combined trumps[1].

Count Tricks

When partner makes a preemptive opening bid, responder can estimate the likely number of playing tricks in partner's hand as one fewer than the number of cards in partner's long suit.

- If partner opens a weak two-bid, showing a six-card suit, responder can estimate partner holds about five playing tricks.

- If partner opens a three-level preemptive bid, showing a seven-card suit, responder can estimate partner holds about six playing tricks.

- If partner opens a four-level preemptive bid, showing an eight-card suit, responder can estimate partner holds about seven playing tricks.

Responder then adds the number of expected playing tricks in responder's hand to those shown by opener to determine if there are likely to be enough for game.

---

[1] This is derived as a competitive conclusion based on the *Law of Total Tricks*.

For example, suppose North opens 3♠, East passes, and it's South's *call*.

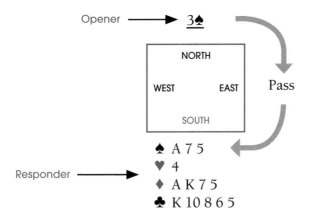

Opener ———▶ <u>3♠</u>

NORTH

WEST   EAST   Pass

SOUTH

♠ A 7 5
♥ 4
Responder ———▶ ♦ A K 7 5
♣ K 10 8 6 5

4♠. With three-card *support* for North's spades, South expects North has a chance of taking ten tricks. South counts three *sure tricks*, the ♠A and ♦A-K. North will be able to trump a second round of hearts with a small spade in the South hand – the dummy – to gain a trick. North may even be able to trump more than one heart in the dummy. So, the partnership should go for the *game bonus*. North has about six playing tricks and South can likely contribute four tricks, for a total of ten tricks.

Consider this example. North opens with a weak 2♥ bid, East passes, and South, as responder, has to decide HOW HIGH and WHERE.

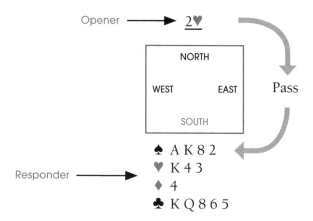

4♥. With three-card support for North's hearts, South can go for the game bonus because there should be the possibility to take ten tricks. The ♠A, ♠K, ♥K, and ♣K-Q combination should each provide a trick. In addition, North may be able to gain a trick or two by *trumping* diamonds in the South hand, the dummy, since South has only one diamond. Opener is showing about five tricks, so the partnership should have a good chance for ten tricks.

Count Trumps

If there are not enough combined tricks for game, responder considers raising opener's suit as a further preemptive action. There may be so little combined strength it is likely the opponents can make a game or even a *slam*. Responder uses the following guideline:

> ### Law of Total Tricks Guideline
>
> Compete to the level corresponding to the number of combined trumps.

Raising opener's preempt when holding a suitable *fit* can make it more challenging for the opponents to find their best contract. Therefore:

- If the partnership has eight combined trumps, responder can compete to the eight-trick level, the two level.
- If the partnership has nine combined trumps, responder can compete to the nine-trick level, the three level.
- If the partnership has ten combined trumps, responder can compete to the ten-trick level, the four level.

Consider this example. North opens 3♠, East passes, and it's South's call.

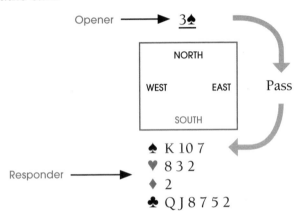

4♠. Here South raises to game out of weakness rather than strength. South doesn't expect the partnership to take ten tricks. However, since North has shown a weak hand with little or no strength outside the spade suit, it's likely the opponents can make at least a *game contract* and maybe a slam if given enough room to find their best spot. By raising to 4♠, South hopes to take away more bidding room from the opponents. They might now bid too much or too little.

Even though the 4♠ contract will probably be defeated, the opponents' score is likely to be less than the score they would get for bidding and making their game or slam contract. South is making a *sacrifice*.

Let's look at another example:

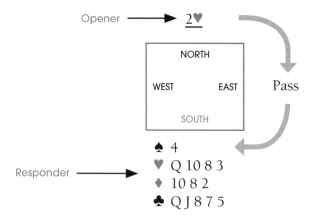

Opener ⟶ 2♥

NORTH

WEST   EAST   Pass

SOUTH

Responder ⟶
♠ 4
♥ Q 10 8 3
♦ 10 8 2
♣ Q J 8 7 5

4♥. South doesn't expect the partnership to have enough combined strength to take ten tricks. However, since North has shown a weak hand with little or no strength outside the heart suit, it's likely the opponents can make at least a game contract and maybe a slam if given enough room to find their best spot. North has shown six hearts and South has four-card support. South counts the combined trumps and competes to the appropriate level: ten trumps equals the ten-trick level.

South would make the same call even if East entered the auction.

Responder's Other Options

Although opener's preemptive bid shows a good long suit and responder's priority is to consider raising with enough tricks for game or enough trumps to compete further, responder has other options. Responder can:

- Pass.
- Bid a *new suit*.
- Bid notrump.

Pass

When responder doesn't have a fit for opener's suit and doesn't have enough strength to consider going for game, responder can simply pass and leave opener to play in the long suit. Since opener is showing a weak hand, responder may often have to pass even with the values for an opening one-level bid or more.

Suppose North opens 3♠, East passes, and it's South's call with this hand.

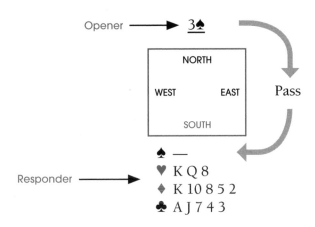

Pass. North probably has no more than six playing tricks and South, even with 13 high-card points plus 1 point for the length in diamonds and 1 point for the length in clubs, can't contribute enough tricks to make a game contract. Don't consider playing in notrump with no fit for partner's suit. North will get several tricks with spades as the trump suit, but may be unable to provide a single trick in a notrump contract. Since South has no spades, there may be no *link card* to reach North's hand.

Responder shouldn't try to improve the contract by bidding a new suit. This will get the partnership higher on the bidding ladder and likely into more trouble.

In this next example, North opens 2♠, East passes, and it's South's call.

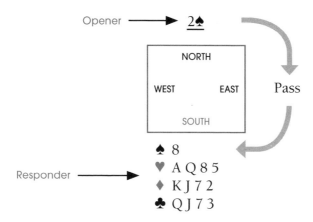

Pass. South has 13 high-card points, enough to open the bidding, but not the values to take the partnership any higher after North's 2♠ bid. North has less than the values for an opening bid – and only about five playing tricks – so there won't be enough combined strength to consider going for a game bonus. The only sure trick South can provide is the ♥A. High cards such as the ♥Q, ♦K-J, and ♣Q-J might provide a couple of tricks, but there is no guarantee. Hopefully, South can contribute enough strength for North to take eight tricks in the 2♠ contract.

South shouldn't consider playing in notrump with no fit for partner's suit. North's six-card suit will take several tricks if spades are trumps, but won't provide many tricks in a notrump contract. Even if South could *establish* some winning tricks in partner's spade suit, there would be difficulty getting to them. North will have little or no strength outside the spade suit.

Bid a New Suit

Although opener's preemptive bid strongly suggests playing with opener's suit as trumps, responder may have other ideas.

Responder might want to suggest another suit as trumps. As with responding to an opening bid in a suit at the one level, responder's bid of a new suit below the game level is *forcing*. Opener is expected to make a further descriptive bid.

Partner, sitting North, opens 2♦. East passes. It's South's call.

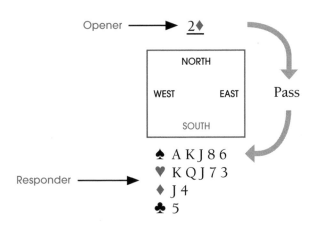

2♠. Responder has 15 high-card points plus 1 length point for each five-card suit. Responder is strong enough the partnership may belong in game even though opener is showing less than the values for a one-level opening bid. Although opener has suggested diamonds as trumps, the partnership could belong in another suit. If opener has either three spades or three hearts, the partnership will have an eight-card *major-suit* fit.

Responder can start by bidding 2♠, a new suit, forcing. With three-card support for spades, or perhaps a strong *doubleton*, opener can raise. If opener doesn't like spades and returns to 3♦, responder can bid the second suit, 3♥. Since this is a new suit below the game level, it is still forcing, asking for a further description from opener.

If opener doesn't like hearts either and bids 4♦, responder can put the partnership in game in 5♦. Hopefully, the only tricks lost will be a club and a heart.

Suppose North is the dealer and opens with a weak 3♣ bid. East passes, and it's South's call.

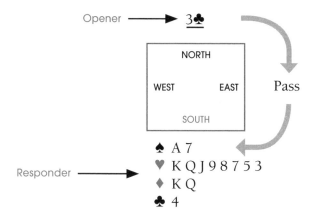

4♥. With an eight-card heart suit and a strong hand, responder knows both How High and Where the partnership belongs. Responder can simply jump to game in 4♥. Although this is a new suit, it is at the game level, so opener is expected to pass.

Bid Game in Notrump

When opener preempts in a *minor suit*, game in the minor suit requires eleven tricks. When responder has enough to take the partnership to game, it might be better to play game in notrump, which requires only nine tricks.

Suppose North opens 3♦ and East passes. It's South's call.

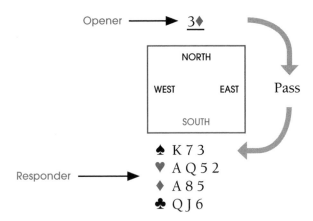

3NT. Although responder has three-card support for diamonds, there may not be enough tricks to make 5♦. Opener is showing only about six playing tricks and responder has only a couple of sure tricks.

Responder can bid 3NT. With a fit for diamonds, there will likely be seven diamond tricks, a heart trick, and a ninth trick coming from whichever suit the opponents lead.

Responder might also suggest playing game in 3NT with no fit for opener's suit but a long running suit that may produce enough tricks.

Suppose North is the dealer and opens a weak two-bid, 2♥. East passes, and it's South's call.

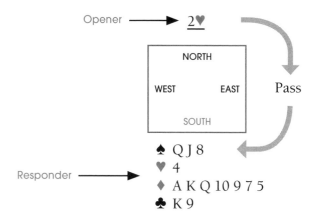

3NT. Responder doesn't have a fit for opener's suit but likely has seven diamond tricks. Responder can expect to get an eighth trick when the opponents lead a spade or a club. If North can provide one trick, the partnership can make game in 3NT. That should be better than trying for ten tricks in hearts or eleven tricks in diamonds.

The Artificial 2NT

When opener starts with a weak two-bid, responder may be unsure How High and Where the partnership belongs. A response of 2NT has a special – *conventional* – meaning. It asks for a further description of opener's hand.

- With a minimum of about 5-8 points, opener can simply *rebid* the suit at the three level.

- With more than a minimum, opener can bid a new suit to show a *feature* in that suit, such as an ace or king, or bid 3NT with a near-solid suit but no outside feature.

Suppose North opens a weak 2♦ and East passes. It's South's call.

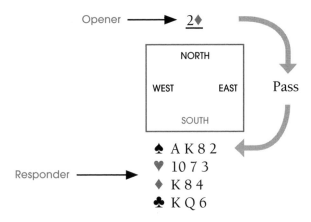

2NT. Responder has enough to try for game. With a diamond fit, there might be nine tricks in 3NT except there is danger because of the weak heart holding. If North has a maximum, the partnership might make 5♦; if not, the partnership may want to stop in *partscore*. Responder can bid 2NT, artificial, to ask for a further description from opener.

If opener shows a feature in hearts, responder can now try 3NT, being less worried about the heart suit. If opener returns to 3♦, showing a minimum, responder can pass and settle for partscore.

Opener's Role After Preempting

A preemptive opening bid gives an accurate description and leaves further decisions for the partnership up to responder. Opener doesn't bid again if responder raises or bids game. Opener only makes another bid if responder makes a forcing bid, such as a new suit below game or the artificial 2NT response.

Scoring

There are three ways to score points:

- *Trick score*.
- *Bonuses*.
- *Penalties*.

Trick Score

The points awarded for each trick bid and made depend on the *denomination* of the contract:

- In notrump: 40 points for the first trick and 30 points for each subsequent trick.
- In the major suits, hearts or spades: 30 points per trick bid and made.
- In the minor suits, clubs or diamonds: 20 points per trick bid and made.

If a side bids and makes a 2♥ contract, for example, the trick score is 60 points (30 + 30). A 3NT contract is worth a trick score of 100 (40 + 30 + 30).

Game Bonuses

A contract with a trick score of 100 or more points is awarded a game bonus. Game can be scored in a single *deal* by bidding and making the following game contracts:

- Eleven or more tricks in a minor suit, 5♣ or 5♦.
- Ten or more tricks in a major suit, 4♥ or 4♠.
- Nine or more tricks in notrump, 3NT.

A factor called *vulnerability* impacts the bonuses awarded for bidding and making contracts. On each deal:

- Neither side may be designated as *vulnerable*.
- Only one side may be designated as vulnerable.
- Both sides may be designated as vulnerable.

In *duplicate* bridge, a popular form of the game, vulnerability is pre-assigned on each deal.

Bonuses for bidding and making the contract are awarded as follows:

- 500 points for a vulnerable game.
- 300 points for a *non-vulnerable* game.
- 50 points for a partscore – a non-game contract.

Overtricks

Tricks made beyond those required to fulfill the contract are called *overtricks*. They are added to the trick score after any bonuses have been awarded at the same rate as the regular trick score:

- In notrump: 30 points per overtrick.
- In hearts or spades: 30 points per overtrick.
- In clubs or diamonds: 20 points per overtrick.

For example, if the partnership bids to a contract of 2♠ and takes ten tricks, it is awarded 170 points: a trick score of 60 (30 + 30), a 50 point partscore bonus, plus 60 for overtricks (30 +30).

If the partnership is vulnerable and bids to a contract of 3NT and takes 10 tricks, it is awarded 630 points: a trick score of 100 (40 + 30 + 30), a 500 point vulnerable game bonus, plus 30 points for the overtrick.

There are additional bonuses awarded for bidding and making a *small slam* – twelve tricks – or a *grand slam* – all thirteen tricks. These are discussed in more detail in Appendix 2.

Penalty Points

If declarer doesn't take the required number of tricks, the opponents receive points for each trick by which the contract is defeated – each *undertrick*. The *penalty* depends on the vulnerability of the declaring side:

- 100 points each undertrick when vulnerable.
- 50 points each undertrick when non-vulnerable.

If a non-vulnerable 3♣ contract is defeated three tricks, the defenders get 150 points (50 + 50 + 50). If a vulnerable 4♥ contract is defeated two tricks, the defenders get 200 points (100 + 100).

When the opponents don't think declarer can make the contract, they can *double* the contract to increase the penalty if the contract is defeated:

- Doubled penalty non-vulnerable: 100 points for the first, 200 for the second and third undertrick, and 300 per trick thereafter.
- Doubled penalty vulnerable: 200 points for the first, and 300 points per trick thereafter.

Doubles are discussed in Chapter 3. They can be effective as a deterrent to preempting too high, especially when vulnerable.

When playing online, the scores are automatically calculated.

There is a handy Scoring Chart available in the Appendix.

Requirements for Preemptive Opening Bids

- Less than the values for an opening bid at the one level.
- A good six-card suit in diamonds, hearts, or spades at the two level.
- A good seven-card suit at the three level.
- A good eight-card suit at the four level.

Responding to a Preemptive Opening

When responding to a preemptive opening, focus on the trick-taking potential of the *combined hands* instead of the high-card points.

- Pass with no fit for opener's suit and little prospect of making a game contract.
- Raise opener's suit in two situations:
  - When the partnership is likely to be able to take enough tricks to make a game contract.
  - When you have support for opener's suit but a weak hand, and it is likely the opponents can make at least a game contract.
- When you are interested in reaching game but are unsure HOW HIGH and WHERE the partnership belongs:
  - Bid a new suit (forcing) to see if opener has support.
  - Bid 2NT after a weak two-bid to ask for more information.

Rebids by the Preemptive Opener

- Pass unless responder makes a forcing call such as a new suit or artificial 2NT.

Quiz – Part I

What call would South make with the following hands?

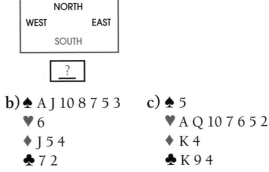

a) ♠ 8 5
♥ 7 4
♦ 6 2
♣ K Q J 9 7 5 3

b) ♠ A J 10 8 7 5 3
♥ 6
♦ J 5 4
♣ 7 2

c) ♠ 5
♥ A Q 10 7 6 5 2
♦ K 4
♣ K 9 4

d) ♠ Q 4
♥ Q 9 3
♦ 9 8 7 6 4 3 2
♣ J

e) ♠ 9
♥ 3
♦ K J 10 8 7 5 4
♣ J 10 7 2

f) ♠ Q 10 9 7 5 4 3
♥ 8
♦ 8 7 5
♣ J 6

North is the dealer. North opens 3♥ and East passes. What call would South make?

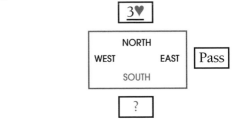

g) ♠ K 9 7
♥ 4
♦ A J 8 2
♣ Q 10 7 5 3

h) ♠ A J 7 3
♥ K 9 4
♦ A K
♣ 7 5 4 3

i) ♠ K J 7 6 5 3
♥ —
♦ Q 10 8 3
♣ A 9 5

j) ♠ A Q 10 7 5 4 2
♥ 3
♦ K Q J
♣ A Q

k) ♠ 9 8 6
♥ Q 10 7 3
♦ 4 3
♣ K 9 7 6

l) ♠ K J 7 4
♥ 8
♦ K Q 6 2
♣ A J 7 5

a) 3♣. With a good seven-card suit and less than the values for an opening bid at the one level, South can open with a preemptive bid.

b) 3♠. The suit isn't solid but has three of the top five cards. South can expect to take five or six tricks with this suit, so an opening bid of 3♠ is reasonable.

c) 1♥. South has a good seven-card suit but also has 12 high-card points plus 3 length points for the seven-card suit. With a hand that values 12 or more points, South opens at the one level.

d) Pass. South has a weak hand and a seven-card suit, but the suit doesn't have any top honors. It would be too risky to open a preemptive bid.

e) 3♦. The diamond suit is good enough it should provide at least five tricks even if South has to lose to the ♦A and ♦Q. The club suit might also provide a trick through length. Opening 3♦ is a practical bid.

f) Pass. This is a close decision. Some players might open 3♠ but it is risky with a suit of this quality. Still, it could work well.

g) Pass. South has only one sure trick. The partnership is high enough.

h) 4♥. North should have about six playing tricks. South's ♠A, ♥K, and ♦A-K should provide enough tricks to make game.

i) Pass. North should have more hearts than South has spades. Bidding is unlikely to improve the contract.

j) 3♠. North may have enough spades to raise. If not, North will rebid 4♥ and South can hope that is the best contract. 3♠ is forcing.

k) 4♥. With an excellent fit for hearts but little else, it is likely East-West can make a game or slam. South raises as a further preemptive action.

l) Pass. South's assortment of high cards might provide some tricks for North but unlikely enough to make a game.

Quiz – Part II

East passes. What call would South make with the following hands?

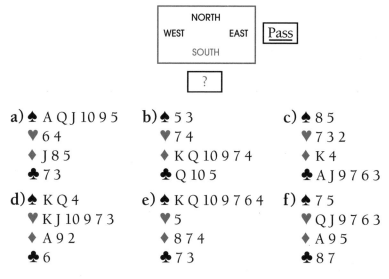

a) ♠ A Q J 10 9 5
   ♥ 6 4
   ♦ J 8 5
   ♣ 7 3

b) ♠ 5 3
   ♥ 7 4
   ♦ K Q 10 9 7 4
   ♣ Q 10 5

c) ♠ 8 5
   ♥ 7 3 2
   ♦ K 4
   ♣ A J 9 7 6 3

d) ♠ K Q 4
   ♥ K J 10 9 7 3
   ♦ A 9 2
   ♣ 6

e) ♠ K Q 10 9 7 6 4
   ♥ 5
   ♦ 8 7 4
   ♣ 7 3

f) ♠ 7 5
   ♥ Q J 9 7 6 3
   ♦ A 9 5
   ♣ 8 7

North opens 2♥ and East passes. What call would South make?

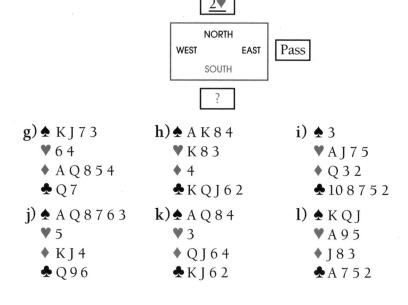

g) ♠ K J 7 3
   ♥ 6 4
   ♦ A Q 8 5 4
   ♣ Q 7

h) ♠ A K 8 4
   ♥ K 8 3
   ♦ 4
   ♣ K Q J 6 2

i) ♠ 3
   ♥ A J 7 5
   ♦ Q 3 2
   ♣ 10 8 7 5 2

j) ♠ A Q 8 7 6 3
   ♥ 5
   ♦ K J 4
   ♣ Q 9 6

k) ♠ A Q 8 4
   ♥ 3
   ♦ Q J 6 4
   ♣ K J 6 2

l) ♠ K Q J
   ♥ A 9 5
   ♦ J 8 3
   ♣ A 7 5 2

a) 2♠. With 8 high-card points plus 2 length points for the six-card suit, South doesn't have enough to open at the one level but can open with a weak two-bid.

b) 2♦. With a good six-card suit and only 7 high-card points, South can open with a weak two-bid in diamonds to describe the hand.

c) Pass. Although South has a six-card club suit and not enough strength to open at the one level, South can't open a weak two-bid when clubs is the suit. South passes instead.

d) 1♥. South has a good six-card suit but, with 13 high-card points plus 2 length points, South can open at the one level.

e) 3♠. An opening of 3♠ is appropriate, holding a good seven-card suit and less than the values for an opening bid at the one level.

f) Pass/2♥. This is a borderline decision since the quality of the heart suit is not ideal. Some players would open 2♥; others would pass. It would be easier if the ace were in hearts instead of diamonds.

g) Pass. Although South has enough strength to open the bidding – 12 high-card points plus 1 length point for the five-card suit – there is unlikely to be enough combined playing tricks to make game.

h) 4♥. North should have about five playing tricks with hearts as the trump suit. South's hand should provide about five: two in spades, one in hearts, two in clubs, and North may be able to *ruff* a diamond in the South hand.

i) 4♥. South doesn't expect to make 4♥ but, with such an excellent fit in North's suit and so little strength outside, South wants to make it more challenging for East-West to enter the auction.

j) Pass. South might prefer spades as the trump suit, but there's no guarantee South's spades are better than North's hearts. Also, a 2♠ response would be forcing, likely getting the partnership too high.

k) Pass. Since North is showing a hand too weak to open at the one level, it's unlikely there is enough combined strength for game. A notrump contract is unlikely to be successful since North will have little strength outside the heart suit.

l) 2NT. With enough strength to be interested in reaching a game contract, South can make use of the conventional 2NT response to get further information about North's hand. If North rebids 3♥ to show a minimum weak two-bid, South can pass and settle for partscore. If North bids anything else, South can go for the game bonus.

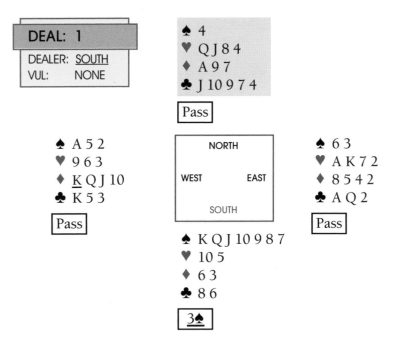

Suggested Bidding

South opens 3♣. South has only 6 high-card points plus 3 length points, not enough to open the bidding at the one level. With a good seven-card suit, however, South can make a preemptive opening bid. This bid is obstructive, taking bidding room from the opponents.

West passes. West has 13 high-card points, enough to open the bidding 1♦, but not enough to start competing at the three level or higher. South's preemptive 3♣ opening interferes with West's bid.

North passes. Although South's bid is obstructive, it's also descriptive. North knows the type of hand South holds. North doesn't like South's choice of trump suit, but knows South has a strong seven-card suit and wants to play with spades as trumps. With only one sure trick, the ♦A, North knows the partnership doesn't have enough combined strength for game.

East passes. East has 13 high-card points, enough to open at the one level. However, South's 3♣ opening has made it awkward for East to enter the auction. East may choose to pass[2]. That would end the auction.

---

[2] East might choose to make a takeout double. This call is discussed in Chapter 3.

If South had passed instead of opening 3♠, East-West would likely get to a 3NT game after an auction like this:

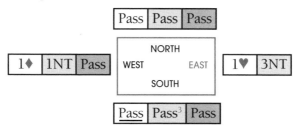

Pass	Pass	Pass

| 1♦ | 1NT | Pass | | | 1♥ | 3NT |

NORTH
WEST   EAST
SOUTH

| Pass | Pass³ | Pass |

In 3NT, East-West have six tricks, the ♠A, ♥A-K, and ♣A-K-Q, and can *promote* three diamond tricks. Even if South can promote six spade *winners*, there is no way South can gain the lead to take them.

Suggested Opening Lead

Against South's 3♠ contract, West would lead the ♦K, top of the solid sequence.

Suggested Play

South's goal is nine tricks. There is only one sure trick, the ♦A. Eight more tricks are needed.

So, South moves to the second planning stage and browses Declarer's Checklist. South can plan to develop six winners in the spade suit through promotion. That will provide a total of seven tricks, two short of the goal, but that's the best declarer can do. The contract will be defeated two tricks.

DECLARER'S PLAN—THE ABC'S
Declarer: South   Contract: 3♠
ASSESS THE SITUATION
Goal   9
Sure Tricks   1
Extra Tricks Needed   8
BROWSE DECLARER'S CHECKLIST
Promotion   6 in spades
Length
Finesse
Trumping in dummy
CONSIDER THE ORDER
• *Draw trumps.*

Conclusion

Being defeated two tricks in 3♠ is a good result for North-South. Since North and South are non-vulnerable, the penalty is 100 points (50 per trick). That's much less than the 400 point score East-West would receive for bidding and making 3NT. Even if North-South were doubled in the 3♠ contract, they would lose only 300 points.

---

³ South might enter the auction at this point (see Chapter 2) but East-West are still likely to reach game.

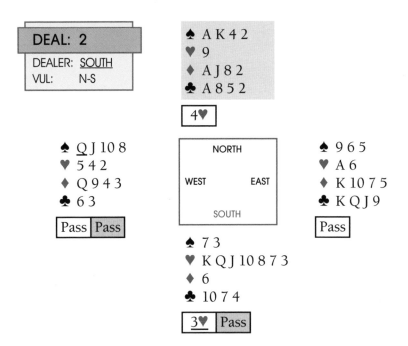

DEAL: 2

DEALER: SOUTH
VUL: N-S

NORTH
♠ A K 4 2
♥ 9
♦ A J 8 2
♣ A 8 5 2

4♥

WEST
♠ Q J 10 8
♥ 5 4 2
♦ Q 9 4 3
♣ 6 3

Pass Pass

EAST
♠ 9 6 5
♥ A 6
♦ K 10 7 5
♣ K Q J 9

Pass

SOUTH
♠ 7 3
♥ K Q J 10 8 7 3
♦ 6
♣ 10 7 4

3♥ Pass

Suggested Bidding

South opens 3♥. With a good seven-card suit but not enough to open the bidding at the one level, South can start the auction with a preemptive opening bid. South's heart suit should produce six tricks.

West passes with only 5 high-card points.

North puts the partnership in the game contract of 4♥. North knows partner has a seven-card heart suit, so hearts should be a good trump suit even though North has only one heart. North also knows South has about six playing tricks. With four sure tricks – the ♠A-K, ♦A, and ♣A – the partnership should be able to take ten tricks.

East passes. With 13 high-card points, East doesn't have enough to enter the auction at the four level. South and West have nothing more to say, so the auction is over.

Suggested Opening Lead

Against South's 4♥ contract, West would lead the ♠Q, top of the solid sequence in an *unbid suit*.

Suggested Play

After West makes the opening lead and the North hand comes down as dummy, South makes a plan. As declarer, South's goal is to take at least ten tricks to make the 4♥ contract. South begins by counting the sure winners: two spades, one diamond, and one club for a total of four tricks. Six more tricks are required.

DECLARER'S PLAN—THE ABC'S	
Declarer: South	Contract: 4♥
ASSESS THE SITUATION	
Goal	10
Sure Tricks	4
Extra Tricks Needed	6
BROWSE DECLARER'S CHECKLIST	
Promotion	6 in hearts
Length	
Finesse	
Trumping in dummy	
CONSIDER THE ORDER	
• Draw trumps.	

Moving to the second stage, South browses Declarer's Checklist. The heart suit will provide six tricks through promotion once the ♥A is driven out.

After winning the first trick with one of dummy's high spades, declarer's priority is to draw the defenders' trumps. Declarer leads dummy's ♥9 and overtakes in the South hand so declarer can continue leading hearts until the ♥A is driven out. On regaining the lead, declarer draws any remaining trumps and it is then safe to take the remaining winners.

Conclusion

North should not consider bidding 3NT with only one heart. South's hand is unlikely to produce many tricks in a notrump contract, but will provide a lot of tricks with hearts as the trump suit.

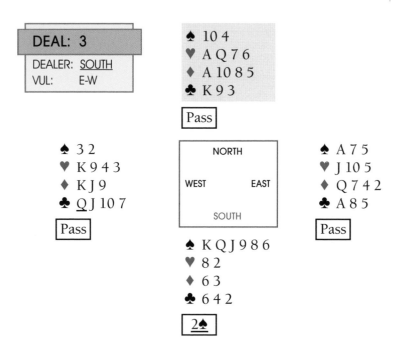

DEAL: 3

DEALER: <u>SOUTH</u>
VUL: E-W

♠ 10 4
♥ A Q 7 6
♦ A 10 8 5
♣ K 9 3

Pass

	NORTH	
WEST		EAST
	SOUTH	

♠ 3 2
♥ K 9 4 3
♦ K J 9
♣ Q J 10 7

Pass

♠ A 7 5
♥ J 10 5
♦ Q 7 4 2
♣ A 8 5

Pass

♠ K Q J 9 8 6
♥ 8 2
♦ 6 3
♣ 6 4 2

2♠

Suggested Bidding

South opens 2♠ as the dealer. With 6 high-card points plus 2 length points, South does not have enough to open the bidding at the one level. With a good six-card suit, however, South can open the bidding with a weak two-bid. South has a reasonable expectation of taking five tricks with spades as trumps.

West passes with only 10 high-card points.

North passes. North has 13 high-card points, but knows there is unlikely to be enough combined strength for a game contract because South has shown less than the values for an opening bid.

East passes, holding only 11 high-card points, not enough to enter the auction. That ends the auction and South becomes declarer in a contract of 2♠.

Suggested Opening Lead

Against South's 2♠ contract, West would lead the ♣Q, top of the solid sequence in an unbid suit.

Suggested Play

When the North hand is put down as dummy, declarer makes a plan. South's goal is to take at least eight tricks. South can count on one sure trick in hearts and one in diamonds. That's a total of two tricks, six short of the goal.

South browses Declarer's Checklist for ways to develop the extra tricks. Five tricks can be promoted in the spade suit. Declarer can hope for an extra trick in hearts by trying the *finesse*. If West holds the ♥K, declarer can lead toward the ♥Q, the card declarer hopes will take a trick.

DECLARER'S PLAN—THE ABC'S	
Declarer: South Contract: 2♠	
ASSESS THE SITUATION	
Goal	8
Sure Tricks	2
Extra Tricks Needed	6
BROWSE DECLARER'S CHECKLIST	
Promotion	5 in spades
Length	
Finesse	1 in hearts
Trumping in dummy	
CONSIDER THE ORDER	
• Draw trumps.	
• Be in the right place at the right time (to lead toward dummy's ♥Q).	

After gaining the lead, declarer can start by leading spades. This has the two-fold effect of promoting winners in the spade suit by driving out the ♠A and of drawing trumps.

After trumps are drawn, it is time for the heart finesse. Declarer needs to be in the South hand to lead a low heart and finesse dummy's ♥Q. As long as West holds the ♥K, declarer will get a trick with both dummy's ♥Q and ♥A.

Conclusion

The weak two-bid immediately gets North-South to their best contract. If East-West enter the auction on this hand, they will get too high and North-South will score points by defeating their contract.

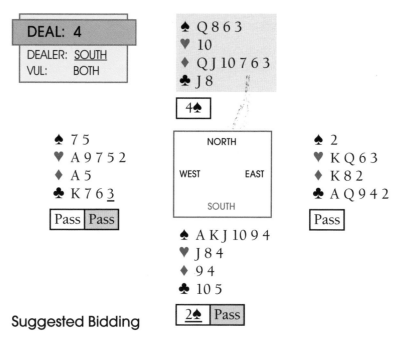

DEAL: 4

DEALER: SOUTH
VUL: BOTH

♠ Q 8 6 3
♥ 10
♦ Q J 10 7 6 3
♣ J 8

4♠

♠ 7 5
♥ A 9 7 5 2
♦ A 5
♣ K 7 6 3

Pass | Pass

NORTH

WEST   EAST

SOUTH

♠ 2
♥ K Q 6 3
♦ K 8 2
♣ A Q 9 4 2

Pass

♠ A K J 10 9 4
♥ J 8 4
♦ 9 4
♣ 10 5

Suggested Bidding

2♠ | Pass

South opens 2♠. South doesn't have enough to open at the one level with only 9 high-card points and 2 length points. However, with a good suit and a reasonable expectation of taking five or six tricks with spades as trumps, South can open with a weak two-bid.

West passes. West has 11 high-card points plus 1 length point for the five-card suit, but West would have to bid at the three level to suggest hearts as trumps and that is too high.

North jumps to 4♠. North has only 6 high-card points but an excellent fit for spades. North can't expect the partnership to take more than seven or eight tricks, but that isn't the only consideration in deciding whether to pass or bid. South has shown a weak hand and North has so little strength it is very likely the opponents have enough strength for at least game. To make it more difficult for East-West to enter the auction, North takes additional preemptive action by jumping to 4♠!

East is now faced with a challenging decision on whether to enter the auction. With 14 high-card points plus 1 length point, East has enough to open at the one level but it might be dangerous to bid at the four level. East might choose to pass[4]. South and West will then pass, ending the auction.

[4] East's options for entering the auction will be discussed in Chapter 3.

Suggested Opening Lead

Against a trump contract, a low card is not usually led from a suit headed by an ace. So, West might choose to lead the ♣3, *fourth highest* in that suit. West might also consider leading the ♥A or ♦A.

Suggested Play

South's goal is to take ten tricks with spades as trumps. South counts six sure tricks in spades, but that's all. Four more tricks need to be developed.

Browsing Declarer's Checklist, there is an opportunity to get two extra tricks by trumping hearts in dummy. Declarer will have to lose one heart trick first.

Suppose the defenders take the first two clubs and then lead a spade. Declarer can win and play a second round of spades to draw the remaining trump, but shouldn't play any more trumps.

DECLARER'S PLAN—THE ABC'S
Declarer: South   Contract: 4♠
ASSESS THE SITUATION
Goal   10
Sure Tricks   6
Extra Tricks Needed   4
BROWSE DECLARER'S CHECKLIST
Promotion
Length
Finesse
Trumping in dummy   2 in hearts
CONSIDER THE ORDER
• Draw trumps.
• Keep two spades in dummy to ruff hearts.

Instead, declarer gives up a heart trick. On regaining the lead, declarer can trump a heart in dummy. After getting back to the South hand, declarer can trump the remaining heart in dummy.

Conclusion

Being defeated two tricks in 4♠ is an excellent result for North-South. East-West can take twelve tricks with either hearts or clubs as the trump suit: five heart tricks, two diamonds, and five clubs. Even if the 4♠ contract is doubled, the penalty of 500 points for being defeated two tricks is less than the value of East-West's potential game or slam contract.

2

Overcalls and the Subsequent Auction

Consider these two auctions. In both cases, East is the dealer. In the first example, East passes. In the second example, East opens 1♣.

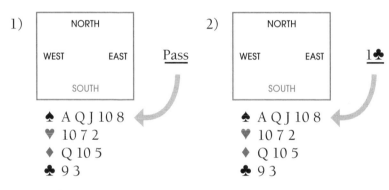

1)

NORTH	
WEST	EAST
SOUTH	

Pass

♠ A Q J 10 8
♥ 10 7 2
♦ Q 10 5
♣ 9 3

2)

NORTH	
WEST	EAST
SOUTH	

1♣

♠ A Q J 10 8
♥ 10 7 2
♦ Q 10 5
♣ 9 3

In the first example, South would not open 1♠ with only 9 high-card points plus 1 length point for the five-card spade suit. An opening bid would describe a hand with 12-21 points.

In the second example, with the same hand, South has to consider the advantages and risks of coming into the auction. One way to compete after the opponents open the bidding is to make a call over the opponent's bid, described as an *overcall*. When both partnerships are bidding for the privilege of naming the trump suit or playing in notrump, it is referred to as a *competitive auction*, and the priorities for both sides can change.

Let's look at the second example again.

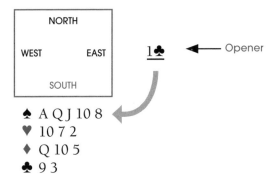

NORTH

WEST   EAST   1♣ ←——— Opener

SOUTH

♠ A Q J 10 8
♥ 10 7 2
♦ Q 10 5
♣ 9 3

Consider the advantages of South's overcall:

- South wants to compete for the contract and prefers spades as trumps.

- A 1♠ overcall could interfere with the opponents' auction. Left to their own devices, the opponents usually settle into their best contract. The 1♠ overcall takes away room on the Bidding Ladder. For example, West can no longer respond 1♦ or 1♥. This may make it more difficult for the opponents to find their best trump fit and to stop at a comfortable level.

- If East-West win the auction, North-South will be defending. By overcalling 1♠, South may help the partnership find the best *defense*. If North has to make the opening lead, for example, South has suggested the spade suit.

There are also risks in overcalling:

- By overcalling, South gives information about the hand to the opponents as well as partner. This might help declarer make better decisions during the play if East-West win the auction.

- If South can't make 1♠, East-West will score points for defeating the contract. East has announced at least 12 points and West is in a good position to judge whether to bid higher or choose to defend and try to defeat the 1♠ contract. East-West could also double for penalties to increase the bonus the partnership receives if North-South can't make the contract.

Requirements for an Overcall

The requirements for making an overcall try to balance the advantages and the risks. Here are some considerations[5].

Suit Quality

The longer and stronger the suit, the safer to overcall since the contract is less likely to be defeated several tricks. Ideally, an overcall shows at least a five-card suit. If the suit is only five cards in length, it's safer to have two of the top three or three of the top five honors.

Hand Valuation

When considering an overcall, the hand is valued the same way as for opening the bidding. Count high-card points: ace, 4; king, 3; queen, 2; jack, 1. Also count length points: 1 point for a five-card suit; 2 points for a six-card suit; and so on.

Level

The risk of overcalling at the one level is minimal compared to the advantages so, with a good suit, an overcall can be made with less than the values for an opening bid. An overcall at the two level or higher, however, carries greater risk, so it tends to show a good suit and strength at least equivalent to that for opening the bidding.

The requirements for making an overcall in a suit are:

The Overcall

DISTRIBUTION: A good five-card suit or a six-card or longer suit.

STRENGTH: 7 to 17[6] points at the one level.

12 to 17 points at the two level or higher.

---

[5] Vulnerability is another consideration. You should be more cautious overcalling when vulnerable since the penalty for being defeated increases.

[6] The upper range for an overcall is lower than for an opening bid. With about 18 or more points, you can start with a takeout double as discussed in Chapter 3.

Hands Meeting Requirements for an Overcall

The following hands are suitable for an overcall after East opens 1♦.

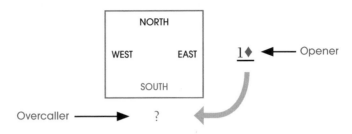

NORTH

WEST   EAST   1♦ ◄—— Opener

SOUTH

Overcaller ——► ?

♠ A Q 10 8 7 5
♥ A J 4
♦ 9 5
♣ K 7

1♠. This is a very sound one-level overcall with 14 high-card points plus 2 length points for the six-card spade suit. South would open 1♠ as dealer. The overcall gets North-South into the auction.

♠ Q J 10 9 8
♥ 8 4
♦ 5 3
♣ A 9 6 4

1♠. This is a minimum one-level overcall. There are only 7 high-card points and South would not open this hand. Still, there is a good five-card suit with three of the top five honors. South would take at least three spade tricks and the ♣A even if North has nothing. The risk in overcalling at the one level is minimal and South would like to compete, to interfere with the opponents, and to suggest a lead.

♠ A 8
♥ K 10 8 7 4 3
♦ 10 6 2
♣ Q 4

1♥. Although the hand is too weak to open the bidding if South were the dealer, there is enough strength for a one-level overcall. The sixth card in hearts makes up for not having three of the top five honors.

♠ A J 9 8 6
♥ 5
♦ J 5
♣ K Q 8 7 3

1♠. With two five-card suits, South overcalls the higher-ranking, the same choice as when opening the bidding. Although the spade suit does not have three of the top five honors, the second five-card suit provides compensation.

Hands Not Meeting Requirements for an Overcall

The following hands are unsuitable for an overcall by South after East opens 1♥.

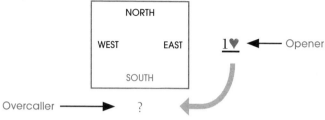

♠ J 7 6 3 2
♥ Q 8 4
♦ K J 3
♣ 5 2

Pass. South has a five-card suit but, with a weak hand and a weak suit, there is little to be gained by overcalling. The risk of being defeated several tricks is substantial.

♠ Q J 5
♥ A J 9 8 4
♦ K 3
♣ Q 5 2

Pass. East picked the suit South likes best. South doesn't want to contest the auction in the same suit as East. Since South would be pleased to defend with hearts as trumps, there's no need to bid.

♠ A 7 6
♥ K J 5
♦ Q 7 6
♣ Q J 6 5

Pass. Even though South would open 1♣ with this hand, it's not necessary to overcall after an opponent opens the bidding. Passing is a better choice than overcalling a weak four-card suit at the two level.

♠ 8 5
♥ J 7 4
♦ Q 8 2
♣ A Q 10 7 5

Pass. There is a reasonable five-card club suit, but the hand isn't strong enough for a two-level overcall.

Overcalls at the Two Level or Higher

Simple overcalls at the two level[7] or higher require a good suit and approximately the values for an opening bid or more. Here are hands suitable for a two-level overcall.

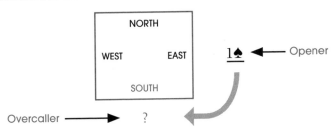

♠ 6 4
♥ 10 3
♦ K 8 2
♣ A K Q 9 6 3

2♣. To overcall at the two level, South needs a good suit and about the same strength as for an opening bid. With 12 high-card points plus 2 length points for the six-card suit, this hand is strong enough to make a two-level overcall.

♠ 6 4
♥ A Q 10 8 3
♦ A K J 8 2
♣ 3

2♥. This is a good hand with enough strength to overcall at the two level. With a choice of suits to overcall, South chooses the higher-ranking.

---

[7] See Practice Deal #30 for an example of an overcall at the three level.

Making an Overcall After Both Opponents Have Bid

The overcall can be used after both opponents have bid. For example, suppose West opens 1♣, North passes, and East responds 1♥. It's South's call.

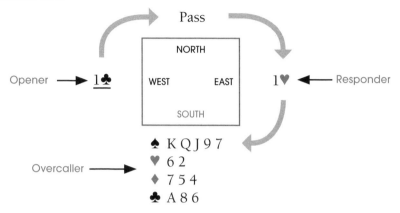

1♠. Now is the time to enter the auction. South has a good five-card suit and 10 high-card points. Although both opponents have bid, North-South may still be able to make a contract. South doesn't want to leave the auction entirely to the opponents.

In this next example, West opens 1♠, North passes, and East raises to 2♠.

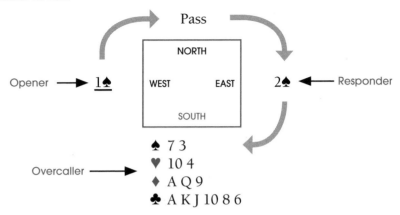

3♣. It's risky to come into the auction at the three level but, with a good six-card suit and a good hand, it's worth the chance. South doesn't want to let the opponents rest at a comfortable level in their chosen trump suit. Maybe South's 3♣ overcall will push East-West higher than they would like to be or buy the contract.

Advancing an Overcall

The partner of the overcaller is referred to as the advancer. The role of advancer is different from that of a player responding to an opening bid. An overcall in either a major or a minor suit, shows a good five-card or longer suit and is a strong suggestion this be the trump suit. This impacts advancer's priorities.

Advancer's Priority – Supporting Partner's Suit

An overcall, in either a major or a minor suit, shows a good five-card or longer suit and is a strong suggestion this be the trump suit. Since overcaller has shown a good five-card suit or longer, *advancer's* priority is to show support with three or more cards in overcaller's suit.

Holding support, advancer values the hand using *dummy points*: *void* – 5; *singleton* – 3; *doubleton* – 1.

Advancing with Minimum Values

As a guideline in competitive auctions, it is usually safe to raise to the level of the combined trumps held by the partnership when holding a weak hand. For example: if the partnership has eight combined trumps, compete to the two level – eight tricks; if the partnership has nine combined trumps, compete to the three level – nine tricks; if the partnership has ten combined trumps, compete to the four level – ten tricks.

This should sound familiar and is in keeping with the concept of bidding to the level corresponding to the combined number of trumps when holding support and a weak hand[8].

Since the overcaller promises at least a five-card suit, advancer can apply this concept to help decide HOW HIGH to raise a one-level overcall with fewer than 10 points:

Advancing a One-Level Overcall with Support and 6-9 Points[9]

- 5-card support   Raise to the game level.
- 4-card support   Raise to the three level.
- 3-card support   Raise to the two level.

---

[8] This is based on The Law of Total Tricks, a theory popularized by Larry Cohen.

[9] 6-9 is only a guideline. Some players will make a preemptive raise with fewer than 6 points.

Here are examples of advancing an overcall with support and about 6-9 points. West opens 1♥, North overcalls 1♠, and East raises to 2♥. It's South's call.

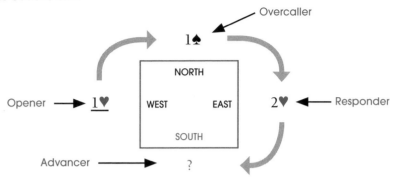

♠ K 8 2
♥ 6 2
♦ K 7 5 4 3
♣ 9 6 2

2♠. With three-card support for overcaller's spade suit and 7 points – 6 high-card points plus 1 dummy point for the doubleton heart – South raises to the two level. South bids 2♠ whether or not East passes or raises to 2♥.

♠ Q J 8 5
♥ 3
♦ Q 7 5 4 3
♣ 9 6 2

3♠. With four-card support for overcaller's spade suit and 8 points – 5 high-card points plus 3 dummy points for the singleton heart – South makes a *preemptive jump raise* to the three level. If North has a minimum overcall and is defeated in this contract, it is likely East-West can make game and North-South have made a good sacrifice.

♠ J 10 8 7 5
♥ —
♦ 10 9 6 4 3
♣ 7 5 2

4♠. It may seem strange to jump to game with only a jack, but that's the recommended strategy for advancer with this type of hand. The hand is worth 6 points: 1 high-card point plus 5 dummy points for the heart void. North is unlikely to make 4♠, but it is very probable East-West can make at least a game and maybe a slam.

Advancing After a Two-Level Overcall with 6-9 Points

For a two-level overcall, partner usually has the equivalent of an opening bid or better. There is less bidding room for the advancer, but the options with 6-9 points are similar to those after a one-level overcall: a single raise shows three-card or longer support; a jump raise is preemptive showing four-card or longer support.

For example, West opens 1♠, North overcalls 2♥, and East raises to 2♠. It's South's call as advancer.

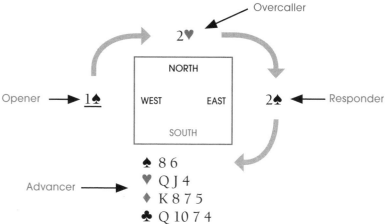

3♥. With 8 high-card points and three-card support for partner's heart suit, South has enough to raise, even though that will get the partnership to the three level. North has shown approximately the values for an opening bid or better by overcalling at the two level, so South wants to compete for the contract in hearts.

Advancing with 10+ Points – The Cuebid

The situation is different when advancer has support and about 10 or more points. Your partnership could expect to make at least a partscore and maybe a game if partner has more than a minimum overcall. Rather than making it difficult for the opponents to reach their best spot, you're trying to reach your best contract.

A jump raise would describe a preemptive hand with 6-9 points and four-card support and might get the partnership too high.

The solution is to make use of a bid available only in a competitive auction, the *cuebid* – a bid of the opponent's suit.

For example, suppose West opens 1♦, North overcalls 1♠, and East passes. A bid of 2♦ by advancer, South, would be a cuebid.

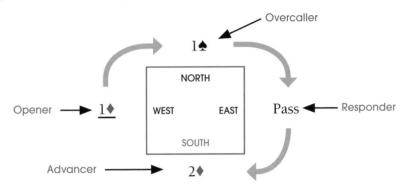

South's 2♦ bid is unlikely to be of much use in a natural sense. South would rarely want to play with diamonds as trumps once West has bid diamonds. It is more practical to use a bid of the opponent's suit for other purposes. The cuebid becomes the tool for advancer to show a hand with support and interest in reaching a game contract, about 10 or more points.

> ### Advancing an Overcall with Support and 10+ Points
>
> Cuebid the opponent's suit,
> showing interest in reaching game.

The cuebid is forcing and the overcaller is expected to bid again if opener passes. With a minimum, North, the overcaller, simply rebids the suit at the cheapest level. With more than a minimum, North makes some other descriptive bid such as a new suit or a jump in the overcalled suit. Advancer can then decide whether to stop in partscore or go for the game bonus.

Here are examples of South advancing an overcall with support and 10+ points after West opens 1♦, North overcalls 1♠, and East passes.

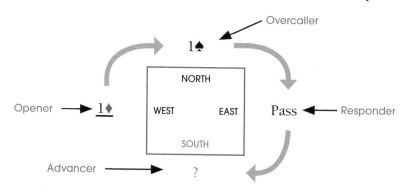

♠ A 7 5
♥ K 9 3
♦ 8 7 5
♣ K J 7 2

2♦. With three-card support for spades and 11 high-card points, South is too strong for a simple raise to 2♠. Start with a 2♦ cuebid, showing interest in reaching game. If North rebids 2♠, South will pass.

♠ K J 8 4
♥ K 3
♦ A 8 6 2
♣ Q 10 7

2♦. With four-card support for overcaller's suit and 14 points – 13 high-card points plus 1 dummy point for the doubleton heart – South shows interest in reaching game by starting with a 2♦ cuebid. If North rebids 2♠, South can make a further try by raising to 3♠. The partnership can still stop short of game if North has a bare minimum overcall of about 7-10 points.

♠ Q 10 8 5
♥ 5
♦ A 10 8 5
♣ A K J 6

2♦. With four-card spade support and 14 high-card points plus 3 dummy points for the singleton heart, South starts with a cuebid. Even if North makes a minimum 2♠ rebid, South has enough to jump to 4♠. South can't bid 4♠ right away because that would be preemptive.

Advancer's Second Choice – A New Suit

Without support for overcaller's suit, advancer can consider bidding a new suit. Since the overcall has already suggested a good five-card or longer suit as the trump suit for the partnership, advancer should introduce another suit only if it is likely to be an improvement. Advancer can use the following guideline:

Guidelines for Advancing in a New Suit

DISTRIBUTION:	A good five-card suit or a six-card or longer suit.
STRENGTH:	6 or more points at the one level.
	11 or more points at the two level.

An advance in a new suit is not forcing[10] since an overcall can be made with less than the values for an opening bid. The partnership doesn't want to get too high in a competitive auction when there isn't a good trump fit.

---

[10] Some partnerships prefer a new suit advance to be forcing. Also, after a two-level or higher overcall, most partnerships would treat a new suit by advancer as forcing.

Here are examples of a new suit advance by South after West opens 1♣, North overcalls 1♥, and East passes.

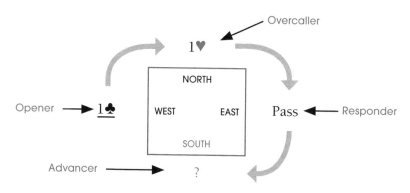

♠ A Q J 10 7
♥ 5 2
♦ Q 8 5 4
♣ 10 7

1♠. South doesn't have support for North's hearts but does have sufficient strength and a good enough suit to suggest spades at the one level. The new suit advance is not forcing. With a minimum overcall, North can pass South's change of suit to avoid getting too high[11].

♠ K 8
♥ J 2
♦ A Q J 8 5 4
♣ 9 8 3

2♦. With 11 high-card points plus 2 length points for the six-card suit, South has enough to bid a new suit at the two level. North may pass with a minimum overcall but that should be fine. The partnership will be high enough.

---

[11] With a very strong hand where you would be disappointed if partner were to pass an advance in a new suit, you can start with a cuebid and then bid your suit.

Advancer's Third Choice – Notrump

With a *balanced hand* and some strength in the opponent's suit, advancer can bid notrump. For example:

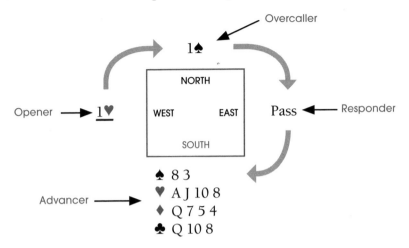

Overcaller

1♠

NORTH

WEST   EAST

SOUTH

Opener ──► 1♥

Pass ◄── Responder

♠ 8 3
♥ A J 10 8
♦ Q 7 5 4
♣ Q 10 8

Advancer ──►

1NT. South doesn't have support for North's spades but does have 9 high-card points and some length and strength in hearts. South can suggest playing in notrump.

```
            Advancing in Notrump

    • 13 or more points    Cuebid
    • 11-12 points         2NT
    • 6-10 points          1NT
```

Passing as Advancer

Advancer doesn't have to bid with no fit for partner's overcalled suit and no good suit to show.

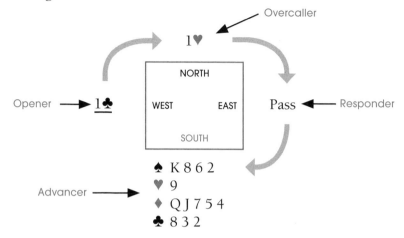

Pass. South has enough to respond if North had opened the bidding, but it's unlikely there is enough combined strength for game. Any attempt to improve the contract may get the partnership further into trouble.

The Overcaller's Rebid

If advancer raises the overcalled suit, bids a new suit, or bids notrump, it's not forcing. The overcaller does not have to bid again. With extra strength or extra *distribution*, however, overcaller can bid again, perhaps moving toward game or bidding game. If advancer cuebids, overcaller must bid again.

Rebids by Overcaller after a Minimum Raise

Advancer's single raise or jump raise shows a minimum hand of about 6-9 points. Overcaller will usually pass but can bid again: With extra strength, it is possible there could be enough combined strength for game. With extra distribution, a six-card suit for example, overcaller can bid again if the opponents are also competing for the contract.

For example, suppose East is the dealer and opens 1♥. South overcalls 1♠, West passes, and North advances to 2♠. East passes.

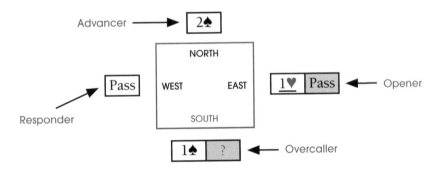

♠ A Q 10 9 5
♥ 8 5 4
♦ K 9 6
♣ J 5

Pass. There are only 11 points – 10 high-card points plus 1 length point for the five-card spade suit – and advancer is showing only 6-9 points. There isn't enough combined strength to consider going for the game bonus.

♠ A K 10 7 5 3
♥ Q 5
♦ A Q 6
♣ 9 4

3♠. This is a strong one-level overcall – 15 high-card points plus 2 length points for the six-card spade suit. So there could be enough combined strength for game if advancer has 8 or 9 points. South can invite game. Advancer, with only 6 or 7 points, can decline the invitation by passing.

Suppose East is the dealer and opens 1♥. South overcalls 1♠, West raises to 2♥, and North advances to 2♠. East now competes to 3♥:

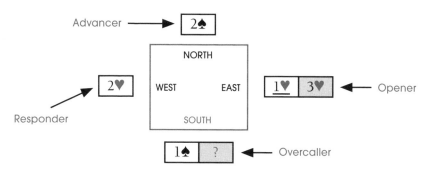

♠ A K 10 7 5 3
♥ 6 5
♦ A 9 4
♣ 9 4

3♠. The choices are passing and defending against 3♥ or competing further. With a good six-card suit, competing to the three level seems reasonable since there should be nine combined trumps – in line with the competitive guideline.

Rebids by Overcaller after a New Suit Advance

Advancer's new suit response is *invitational* but not forcing. It shows a good five-card or longer suit so, with a minimum overcall, you can pass. With extra strength or extra distribution, however, you can bid again.

For example, suppose East is the dealer and opens 1♦. You overcall 1♥, West passes, and partner, North, advances to 1♠. East passes.

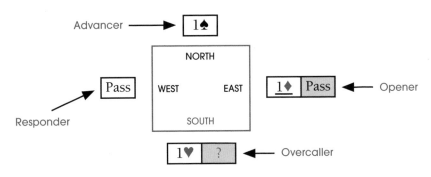

♠ J 4 2
♥ K Q 10 9 5
♦ 9 6
♣ Q 8 2

Pass. North's new suit advance isn't forcing. North hasn't shown support for hearts – which would be advancer's priority with three-card or longer support – and has suggested spades as the trump suit. With a minimum overcall, South can pass and leave the partnership to play partscore in spades.

♠ 3
♥ A Q J 9 7 5
♦ 10 5 3
♣ A 4 2

2♥. South doesn't have to bid again but, with a good six-card heart suit and no support for spades, South can repeat the suggestion the partnership plays with hearts as trumps.

Suppose East is the dealer and opens 1♦. South overcalls 1♥, West passes, and partner, North, advances to 1♠. East now rebids 2♦.

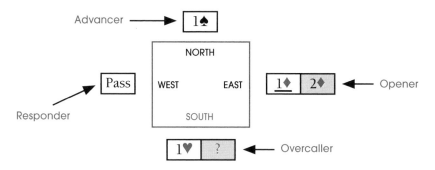

♠ A 10 4
♥ A J 10 7 5
♦ 5 4
♣ K 8 5

2♠. North didn't support South's hearts, but South has support for North's spades. With more than a minimum overcall, South can compete further by raising spades.

Rebids by Overcaller after a Notrump Advance

When advancer bids 1NT or 2NT, it is invitational but not forcing. With a minimum hand, overcaller can pass. With extra strength or extra distribution, however, overcaller can bid again.

For example, suppose East is the dealer and opens 1♣. South overcalls 1♠, West passes, and North advances to 1NT. East passes.

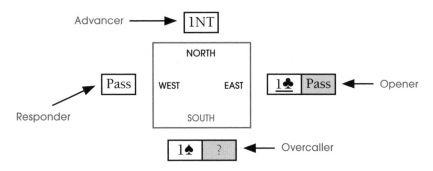

♠ K J 10 8 5
♥ A 9 3
♦ J 6 3
♣ 7 4

Pass. Advancer didn't support South's spades but did show about 6-10 points with some strength in clubs. With a minimum overcall, South can pass. A partscore in notrump looks like the best spot.

♠ A Q 10 5 2
♥ 6 3
♦ K J 10 7 5
♣ 8

2♦. North didn't support spades, South's first suggested trump suit, but does have about 6-10 points. With an *unbalanced hand* unsuitable for notrump, South can show the second suit. North might prefer diamonds to spades.

Rebids by Overcaller after a Cuebid

Advancer's cuebid is forcing, showing interest in reaching game and asking for more information about overcaller's hand. With a minimum, overcaller rebids as cheaply as possible.

Suppose East is the dealer and opens 1♥. South overcalls 1♠, West passes, and North advances to 2♥. East passes.

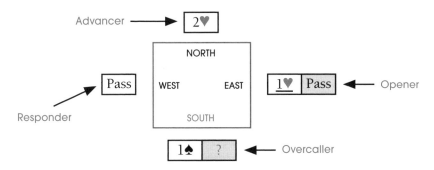

♠ K Q J 8 3
♥ J 9 5
♦ Q 7 2
♣ 9 4

2♠. With nothing extra for the overcall, South rebids spades as cheaply as possible after advancer's cuebid, even though it is only a five-card suit. Advancer likely has support for spades unless advancer is planning to bid something else.

With a medium-strength hand after advancer's cuebid, overcaller makes a forward-going bid such as a new suit or a jump rebid in the original suit.

Suppose East is the dealer and opens 1♣. South overcalls 1♥, West passes, and North advances to 2♣. East passes.

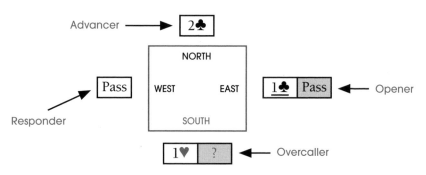

♠ 8 3
♥ A K J 9 5
♦ K Q 7 2
♣ 9 4

2♦. This is a sound one-level overcall with 13 high-card points plus 1 length point for the five-card heart suit. With North showing about 10 or more points, South is interested in reaching game. South can describe the hand further by showing the second suit. Since South didn't simply rebid hearts, this tells advancer South has more than a minimum overcall.

With a maximum-strength hand after advancer's cuebid, overcaller makes sure the partnership gets to game.

Suppose East is the dealer and opens 1♦. South overcalls 1♠, West passes, and North advances to 2♦. East passes.

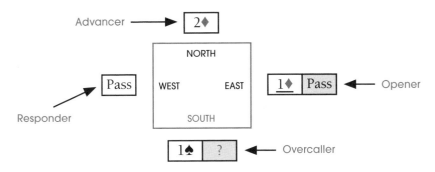

♠ A K J 10 8 7 4   4♠. Since advancer has about 10 or more points
♥ 8 3   for the cuebid and interest in reaching game,
♦ 6   and South has 17 points – 14 high-card points
♣ A Q 9   plus 3 length points for the seven-card suit –
South is willing to go for the game bonus.

Other Overcalls

The Notrump Overcall

Consider South's call with this hand after East opens 1♥.

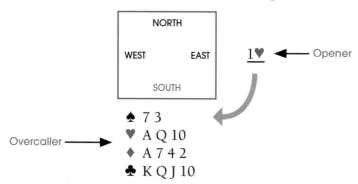

NORTH

WEST   EAST

SOUTH

1♥ ← Opener

Overcaller →

♠ 7 3
♥ A Q 10
♦ A 7 4 2
♣ K Q J 10

1NT. South would have opened 1NT if East had passed. An overcall of 1NT is similar to a 1NT opening bid. It shows a balanced hand of about 15-18 points[12].

The only consideration is East's 1♥ opening showed a five-card or longer suit and West is likely to lead a heart against South's notrump contract. So, South should have some strength in the opponent's suit to overcall 1NT.

Since the 1NT overcall is similar to a 1NT opening bid, advancer can bid in the same manner as responding to a 1NT opening bid.

---

[12] Since there is more risk in overcalling 1NT after an opponent has shown strength by opening the bidding, the upper range is slightly stronger than for a 1NT opening bid. See Practice Deal #26 for an example of a 1NT overcall.

For example, suppose West opens 1♦, North overcalls 1NT, East passes, and it's South's call.

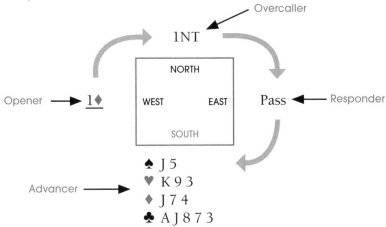

3NT. South has 10 high-card points plus 1 length point for the five-card suit. That's enough to take the partnership to game opposite North's 1NT overcall since the partnership has at least 26 combined points.

The Weak Jump Overcall

A *jump overcall* – bidding one or more levels higher than necessary – is similar to a preemptive opening bid. It shows a weak hand with a long suit[13]. Consider South's call with this hand after East opens 1♦.

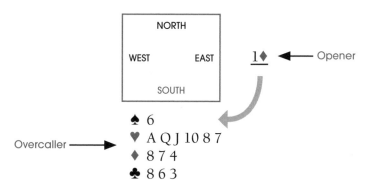

2♥. With a good six-card suit but a hand too weak to open at the one level, South would have opened 2♥, a weak two-bid, if East had passed. So, instead of making a simple 1♥ overcall, South can make a 2♥ preemptive jump overcall.

Like the weak two-bid, the advantage of the weak jump overcall is it takes up room on the Bidding Ladder, making it more challenging for the opponents to find their best contract. Since there is the risk of being doubled for penalty, the hand should be worth about five or six playing tricks.

---

[13] See Practice Deals #27 and #28 for examples of the effect of a weak jump overcall.

With a seven-card suit, a weak jump overcall can be made at the three level, similar to a three-level preemptive opening bid. For example, consider South's call with this hand after East opens 1♠.

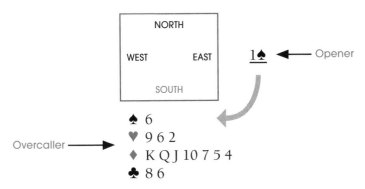

3♦. With a good seven-card suit, South would have opened 3♦ if East had passed. South can make the same call after East opens 1♠, but it is now a weak jump overcall instead of a preemptive three-level opening bid.

As with any preemptive bid, South should be more cautious when vulnerable since the potential penalty is larger. With only six playing tricks, South might prefer to pass with this hand when vulnerable. South shouldn't make a simple 2♦ overcall since North would expect South to hold a stronger hand for a simple two-level overcall – about the values for an opening bid.

SUMMARY

Requirements for a Simple Overcall

Distribution: A good five-card suit or a six-card or longer suit.
Strength: 7 or more points at the one level.
12 or more points at the two level or higher.

Advancing an Overcall with Support

6-9 points: With 3-card support, raise to the cheapest level.
With 4-card support, raise to the three level.
With 5-card support, raise to the game level.
10+ points: Cuebid the opponent's suit, showing interest in reaching game.

Advancing in a New Suit

Distribution: A good five-card suit or a six-card or longer suit.
Strength: 6 or more points at the one level; 11 or more points at the two level.
A new suit advance is not forcing[14].

Advancing in Notrump

6-10 points: Bid notrump at the cheapest level.
11-12 points: Jump in notrump.
13+ points: Cuebid then bid notrump.

Requirements for a 1NT Overcall

Distribution: Balanced hand.
Strength: 15–18 points (some strength in the opponent's suit).

Requirements for a Preemptive Jump Overcall

Distribution: A good six-card suit at the two level.
A good seven-card suit at the three level.
Strength: A weak hand.

[14] Some partnerships prefer to treat a new suit response as forcing.

Quiz – Part I

East opens 1♥. What call would South make with the following hands?

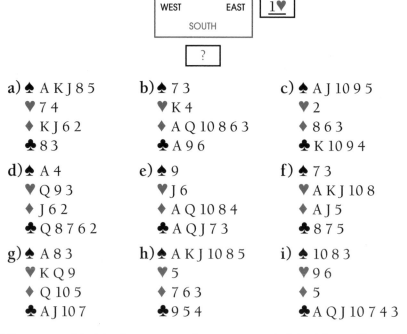

a) ♠ A K J 8 5
♥ 7 4
♦ K J 6 2
♣ 8 3

b) ♠ 7 3
♥ K 4
♦ A Q 10 8 6 3
♣ A 9 6

c) ♠ A J 10 9 5
♥ 2
♦ 8 6 3
♣ K 10 9 4

d) ♠ A 4
♥ Q 9 3
♦ J 6 2
♣ Q 8 7 6 2

e) ♠ 9
♥ J 6
♦ A Q 10 8 4
♣ A Q J 7 3

f) ♠ 7 3
♥ A K J 10 8
♦ A J 5
♣ 8 7 5

g) ♠ A 8 3
♥ K Q 9
♦ Q 10 5
♣ A J 10 7

h) ♠ A K J 10 8 5
♥ 5
♦ 7 6 3
♣ 9 5 4

i) ♠ 10 8 3
♥ 9 6
♦ 5
♣ A Q J 10 7 4 3

West opens 1♠, North passes, and East responds 2♦. What call would South make with the following hands?

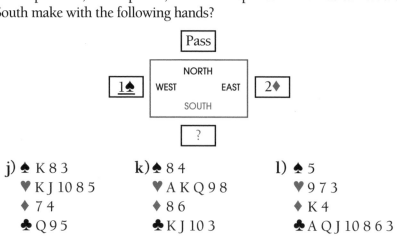

j) ♠ K 8 3
♥ K J 10 8 5
♦ 7 4
♣ Q 9 5

k) ♠ 8 4
♥ A K Q 9 8
♦ 8 6
♣ K J 10 3

l) ♠ 5
♥ 9 7 3
♦ K 4
♣ A Q J 10 8 6 3

---

a) 1♠. With a good five-card spade suit and 12 high-card points, make a simple overcall at the one level.

b) 2♦. With 13 high-card points and a good six-card diamond suit, this hand is strong enough for a simple overcall at the two level.

c) 1♠. Although there are only 8 high-card points, with a good five-card spade suit, that's enough to make a simple overcall at the one level.

d) Pass. With 9 high-card points and a poor five-card suit which would have to be bid at the two level, this hand is unsuitable for an overcall.

e) 2♦. With 14 high-card points plus 1 length point for each five-card suit, there is enough strength to make a simple overcall at the two level. With two five-card suits, South bids the higher-ranking.

f) Pass. East has a five-card or longer heart suit, so South doesn't want to compete in the same suit. South is happy to defend with hearts as the trump suit.

g) 1NT. With a balanced hand and 16 high-card points, South would have opened 1NT if East had passed. After East opens, South can overcall 1NT to describe the hand. South has some strength in hearts, the opponent's suit, in case that suit is led against a notrump contract.

h) 2♠ (1♠). Although South could overcall 1♠, a weak jump overcall to 2♠ is more descriptive. It shows a good six-card suit but a weak hand, similar to an opening weak two-bid.

i) 3♣. A jump overcall to the three level is also preemptive, similar to an opening bid at the three level. If South were to make a simple overcall of 2♣, North would expect a stronger hand.

j) Pass. South has a good five-card suit but not enough strength to make an overcall at the two level.

k) 2♥. With both East and West bidding, it's a little risky to come into the auction at the two level, but South has a good five-card suit and a good hand. South would certainly like North to lead a heart if East-West buy the contract.

l) 3♣. This time, South has to overcall at the three level. South has a good seven-card suit, so it's not too risky.

West opens 1♦. North overcalls 1♥ and East passes. What call would South make, as advancer, with each of the following hands?

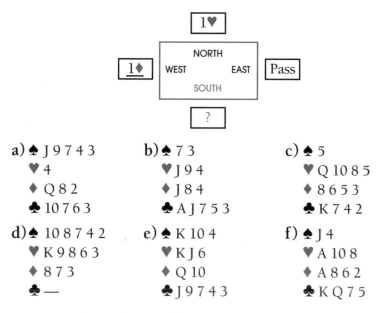

a) ♠ J 9 7 4 3
♥ 4
♦ Q 8 2
♣ 10 7 6 3

b) ♠ 7 3
♥ J 9 4
♦ J 8 4
♣ A J 7 5 3

c) ♠ 5
♥ Q 10 8 5
♦ 8 6 5 3
♣ K 7 4 2

d) ♠ 10 8 7 4 2
♥ K 9 8 6 3
♦ 8 7 3
♣ —

e) ♠ K 10 4
♥ K J 6
♦ Q 10
♣ J 9 7 4 3

f) ♠ J 4
♥ A 10 8
♦ A 8 6 2
♣ K Q 7 5

East opens 1♣, South overcalls 1♠, and West passes. North advances to 2♠ and East passes. What rebid would South make, as the overcaller, with the following hands?

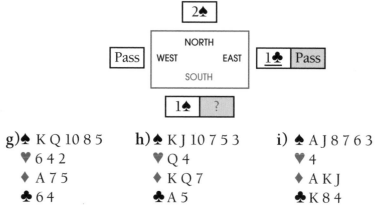

g) ♠ K Q 10 8 5
♥ 6 4 2
♦ A 7 5
♣ 6 4

h) ♠ K J 10 7 5 3
♥ Q 4
♦ K Q 7
♣ A 5

i) ♠ A J 8 7 6 3
♥ 4
♦ A K J
♣ K 8 4

a) Pass. South doesn't like North's choice of trump suit but, with only 3 high-card points plus 1 length point, South doesn't have enough strength to bid another suit or notrump.

b) 2♥. With three-card support for hearts and 7 high-card points plus 1 dummy point for the doubleton spade, South has enough to raise partner's suit.

c) 3♥. South has 5 high-card points plus 3 dummy points for the singleton spade. With a hand in the 6-9 point range and four-card support, South makes a preemptive raise to the three level.

d) 4♥. There are 3 high-card points plus 5 dummy points for the void in clubs. With five-card heart support, South makes a preemptive raise to the game level. If North can't make 4♥, it's likely the opponents can make something.

e) 2♦. With support for partner and 10 high-card points plus 1 dummy point, South cuebids the opponent's suit. If North makes a minimum rebid of 2♥, South can pass. This avoids getting the partnership too high when North has a minimum one-level overcall.

f) 2♦. With support for partner's suit and 14 high-card points plus 1 dummy point for the doubleton spade, South starts with a 2♦ cuebid. If North makes a minimum rebid of 2♥, South can raise to 3♥ to invite partner to bid game.

g) Pass. With 9 high-card points plus 1 length point for the five-card suit, South doesn't have much extra for the overcall. North's raise shows about 6-9 points, so South settles for partscore.

h) 3♠. North has about 6-9 points and South has 15 high-card points plus 2 length points for the six-card suit. Game is possible if North has 8 or 9 points rather than 6 or 7. South invites North to continue to game by rebidding 3♠.

i) 4♠. South has 16 high-card points plus 2 length points for the six-card suit. Even if North has only 7 points, there should be enough combined strength to go for the game bonus.

East opens 1♦, South overcalls 1♠, West passes, North advances to 2♦, and East passes. What does South bid?

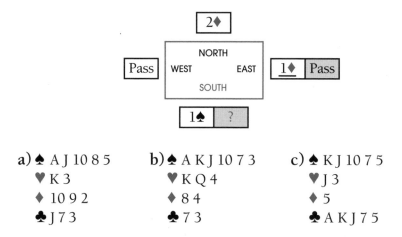

a) ♠ A J 10 8 5
♥ K 3
♦ 10 9 2
♣ J 7 3

b) ♠ A K J 10 7 3
♥ K Q 4
♦ 8 4
♣ 7 3

c) ♠ K J 10 7 5
♥ J 3
♦ 5
♣ A K J 7 5

East opens 1♣, South overcalls 1♥, West passes, North advances to 1♠, and East passes. What is South's call?

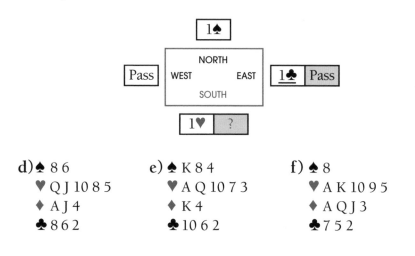

d) ♠ 8 6
♥ Q J 10 8 5
♦ A J 4
♣ 8 6 2

e) ♠ K 8 4
♥ A Q 10 7 3
♦ K 4
♣ 10 6 2

f) ♠ 8
♥ A K 10 9 5
♦ A Q J 3
♣ 7 5 2

a) 2♠. North's 2♦ cuebid of the opponent's suit is forcing, showing 10 or more points. With nothing much extra for the overcall, South rebids spades at the cheapest level.

b) 3♠. With 13 high-card points plus 2 length points for the six-card suit, South has extra strength for the one-level overcall. South can show the extra strength and the extra length in spades by rebidding the suit with a jump.

c) 3♣. North's 2♦ cuebid is forcing. With a good hand for the overcall, South shows the second suit.

d) Pass. A new suit by advancer is not forcing. With nothing extra, South passes and stops in partscore. North should have a good five-card or longer spade suit. Since North didn't raise hearts, North has fewer than three hearts.

e) 2♠. With more than a minimum for the overcall and support for North's spades, South raises to 2♠.

f) 2♦. South doesn't like North's spades but has a good hand for the overcall. South bids the second suit, giving North a choice of hearts or diamonds.

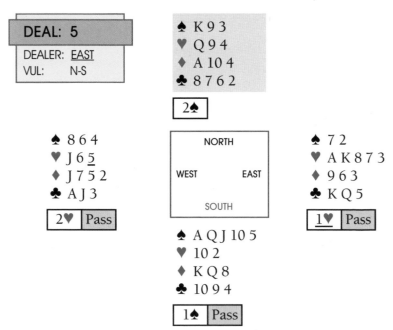

DEAL: 5

DEALER: EAST
VUL: N-S

♠ K 9 3
♥ Q 9 4
♦ A 10 4
♣ 8 7 6 2

2♠

♠ 8 6 4
♥ J 6 5
♦ J 7 5 2
♣ A J 3

2♥ | Pass

NORTH

WEST   EAST

SOUTH

♠ 7 2
♥ A K 8 7 3
♦ 9 6 3
♣ K Q 5

1♥ | Pass

♠ A Q J 10 5
♥ 10 2
♦ K Q 8
♣ 10 9 4

1♠ | Pass

Suggested Bidding

East deals and opens 1♥. East has 12 high-card points plus 1 length point for the five-card heart suit, enough to open the bidding at the one level.

South overcalls 1♠. South has 12 high-card points plus 1 length point for the five-card spade suit. If East had passed, South would open 1♠. After East's opening bid, South can compete for the contract by overcalling 1♠.

West raises to 2♥. West, as responder, has three-card support for East's major suit and 7 high-card points. That's enough to raise to the two level.

North advances to 2♠. North, partner of the overcaller, has 9 high-card points and three-card support for South's suit. North can continue the partnership's competition for the contract by raising to 2♠.

East passes. East has already described the hand by opening the bidding and passes with nothing extra to show.

South passes. Since North's raise is limited to about 9 points, South knows the partnership has only enough combined strength for partscore.

West passes. West has nothing extra to show, having already competed to the two level.

West's pass ends the auction and South is the declarer in 2♠.

Suggested Opening Lead

Against South's 2♠ contract, West would lead the ♥5. With no touching high cards in partner's suit, West leads low from three cards headed by an honor.

Declarer's Plan

After West makes the opening lead and the North hand comes down as dummy, South makes a plan. As declarer, South's goal is to take at least eight tricks to make the 2♠ contract. South begins by counting the sure winners: five sure tricks in spades and three in diamonds. That's a total of eight, exactly what is required.

With enough tricks to make the contract, the priority is to *draw trumps* after gaining the lead. Suppose East wins the first two tricks with the ♥A-K and the defenders then take three club tricks. Whatever the defenders lead next, declarer can win and then start taking spade winners until the defenders have no trumps remaining. This takes three rounds because the five missing trumps are divided 3-2.

DECLARER'S PLAN—THE ABC'S
Declarer: South   Contract: 2♠
ASSESS THE SITUATION
Goal 8
Sure Tricks 8
Extra Tricks Needed 0
BROWSE DECLARER'S CHECKLIST
Not applicable
CONSIDER THE ORDER
• Draw trumps.
• Take the tricks and run.

Once the opponents' trumps are drawn, it is safe to take three diamond winners. On the actual deal, South could have taken the diamond winners before drawing trumps, but that would not have worked if either opponent had a singleton or doubleton diamond.

Conclusion

If North-South did not compete for the contract, East-West would play the contract in 2♥. By using the overcall to compete, North-South will either be left to play in the makeable 2♠ contract or push East-West to 3♥, which can be defeated two tricks.

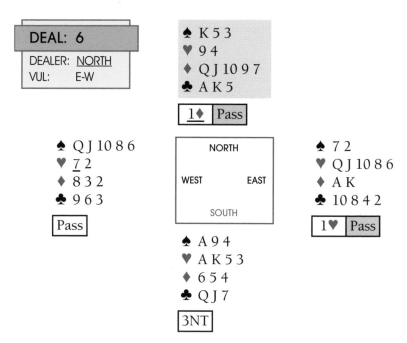

DEAL: 6

DEALER: NORTH
VUL: E-W

♠ K 5 3
♥ 9 4
♦ Q J 10 9 7
♣ A K 5

1♦ | Pass

♠ Q J 10 8 6
♥ 7 2
♦ 8 3 2
♣ 9 6 3

Pass

NORTH

WEST   EAST

SOUTH

♠ 7 2
♥ Q J 10 8 6
♦ A K
♣ 10 8 4 2

1♥ | Pass

♠ A 9 4
♥ A K 5 3
♦ 6 5 4
♣ Q J 7

3NT

Suggested Bidding

North has 13 high-card points plus 1 length point for the five-card diamond suit. North opens in the minor suit, 1♦.

East has only 10 high-card points plus 1 point for the five-card suit but, with a good five-card heart suit and three of the top five honors, East can overcall at the one level.

South, the responder, has a balanced hand with 14 high-card points. Since North has opened the bidding, South decides HOW HIGH, game, knowing the partnership has at least 26 combined points. With strength in hearts, the opponent's suit, South decides WHERE, notrump. South jumps to 3NT.

West, North, and East all pass, and the contract is 3NT played by South.

Suggested Opening Lead

Against South's 3NT contract, West would lead the ♥7, top of the doubleton in partner's suit. If partner hadn't overcalled, West would lead the ♠Q, top of the solid sequence in West's longest suit.

Declarer's Plan

South's goal is to take at least nine tricks to make the 3NT contract. South begins by counting the sure winners: two spades, two hearts, and three clubs, for a total of seven tricks. Two more tricks are needed.

South browses Declarer's Checklist. Declarer can plan to promote three extra winners in the diamond suit by driving out the ♦A and ♦K.

After winning the ♥K, South leads to one of dummy's high diamonds to drive out the ♦K. East wins and leads another heart, driving out South's ♥A. South can lead another high diamond to drive out the ♦A and establish dummy's remaining diamonds as winners.

DECLARER'S PLAN—THE ABC'S	
Declarer: South Contract: 3NT	
ASSESS THE SITUATION	
Goal	9
Sure Tricks	7
Extra Tricks Needed	2
BROWSE DECLARER'S CHECKLIST	
Promotion	3 in diamonds
Length	
Finesse	
CONSIDER THE ORDER	
• Develop the extra diamond tricks early.	

Unfortunately for North-South, East can take enough heart winners to defeat the contract after winning the ♦A. East-West win the race to promote winners in their long suit, thanks to West's opening lead of the ♥7, partner's suit.

Conclusion

If West had led the ♠Q instead of a heart, declarer could make the contract. Declarer wins either the ♠A or ♠K and plays a high diamond to drive out the ♦K. East can lead another spade to drive out declarer's remaining high spade and establish West's remaining spades as winners. When declarer leads another high diamond, however, East wins the ♦A and has no spades to lead. Whatever East leads, declarer wins and takes the established diamond winners to make the contract with an overtrick.

The overcall is effective in getting the partnership off to the best opening lead and did not involve much risk. If North-South choose to defend against 1♥, that contract can only be defeated one trick, for a small penalty. If North-South choose to play in a partscore contract, East's overcall has kept them from getting to 3NT.

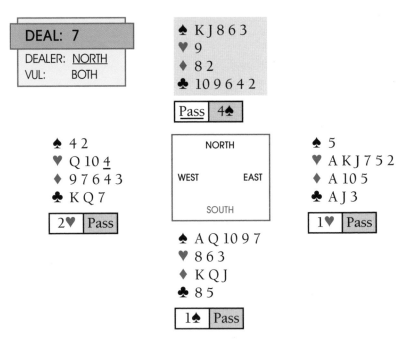

Suggested Bidding

North passes as the dealer. North has only 4 high-card points plus 1 length point for each five-card suit.

East opens 1♥. East has 17 high-card points plus 2 length points for the six-card suit, putting the hand in the top of the 12-21 point range for an opening bid at the one level.

South overcalls 1♠. South has 12 high-card points plus 1 length point for the five-card spade suit. The good five-card suit is more than enough to overcall at the one level.

West raises to 2♥. West has three-card support and 7 high-card points plus 1 dummy point for the doubleton spade.

North advances to 4♠. North has only 4 high-card points but can add 3 dummy points for the singleton heart and 1 dummy point for the doubleton diamond. With five-card support for partner's overcalled suit and a hand in the 6-9 point range, North can make a preemptive raise to the four level. This is a two-way bid. With the good distributional hand, it is likely the partnership can take a lot of tricks with spades as the trump suit. At the same time, the jump to 4♠ makes it difficult for East-West to find their best spot.

East has a challenging decision over North's 4♠ advance. East planned to bid 4♥ but would now have to bid 5♥ to win the contract. That may be too high. East might prefer to defend, hoping to defeat 4♠[15]. If East doesn't bid, South and West will pass and South will become the declarer in 4♠.

Suggested Opening Lead

Against South's 4♠ contract, West would lead the ♥4, low from three or more cards with no touching honors in partner's suit.

Declarer's Plan

South's goal is to take at least ten tricks with spades as trumps. South counts five sure tricks in spades, but that's all. Five more tricks need to be developed.

South browses Declarer's Checklist. Two hearts can be trumped in dummy. Also, two tricks can be promoted in diamonds. That's not enough to make the contract, but it's the best declarer can do.

After East wins the first heart, the defenders may simply take their diamond and club winners. If not, South can draw trumps on gaining the lead, promote the diamond winners, and ruff two hearts with dummy's spades.

DECLARER'S PLAN—THE ABC'S	
Declarer: South	Contract: 4♠
ASSESS THE SITUATION	
Goal	10
Sure Tricks	5
Extra Tricks Needed	5
BROWSE DECLARER'S CHECKLIST	
Promotion	2 in diamonds
Length	
Finesse	
Trumping in Dummy	2 in hearts
CONSIDER THE ORDER	
• Draw trumps.	
• Develop the extra diamond tricks early.	
• Keep two trumps in dummy to ruff hearts.	

Conclusion

Although North-South can't make 4♠, going down one trick is a good result. East-West can make 4♥. They have six heart tricks, a diamond trick, and three club tricks. From North-South's perspective, the penalty for being defeated in 4♠ is less than the score for letting East-West make 4♥.

There's little East-West can do. If East bids 5♥, the contract will be defeated one trick. North's preemptive jump raise is effective.

[15] East might make a penalty double to increase the score for defeating the contract.

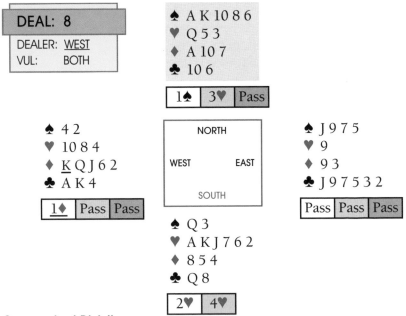

DEAL: 8
DEALER: <u>WEST</u>
VUL: BOTH

♠ A K 10 8 6
♥ Q 5 3
♦ A 10 7
♣ 10 6

| 1♠ | 3♥ | Pass |

NORTH

WEST   EAST

SOUTH

♠ 4 2
♥ 10 8 4
♦ <u>K</u> Q J 6 2
♣ A K 4

| 1♦ | Pass | Pass |

♠ J 9 7 5
♥ 9
♦ 9 3
♣ J 9 7 5 3 2

| Pass | Pass | Pass |

♠ Q 3
♥ A K J 7 6 2
♦ 8 5 4
♣ Q 8

| 2♥ | 4♥ |

Suggested Bidding

West opens 1♦. West has 13 high-card points plus 1 length point for the five-card diamond suit. Although the hand is balanced, it isn't strong enough to open 1NT. With no five-card major, West opens the five-card minor suit.

North overcalls 1♠. North has 13 high-card points plus 1 length point for the five-card spade suit, for a total of 14. With a good five-card suit, North can overcall at the one level.

East passes. East has only 2 high-card points plus 2 length points for the six-card club suit.

South advances 2♥. South doesn't have three-card support for North's spades but does have 12 high-card points plus 2 length points for the six-card heart suit. That's enough to advance in a new suit at the two level. The 2♥ bid is forward-going, but not forcing. North can pass with a minimum overcall.

West passes. West has already opened the bidding and doesn't have enough to bid again.

North raises to 3♥. North has three-card support for South's hearts and more than a minimum for the overcall. North raises to 3♥ to show the support and interest in reaching game.

East passes again, and South now bids 4♥. South has enough to continue to game with the knowledge the partnership has a fit in hearts and North has more than the minimum strength for an overcall. South's 4♥ bid is followed by three passes, ending the auction.

Suggested Opening Lead

Against South's 4♥ contract, West could lead the ♦K, top of the solid sequence, or the ♣A, top of the touching honors in that suit.

Declarer's Plan

South is declarer and the goal is to take ten tricks with hearts as trumps. South counts three sure tricks in spades, six in hearts, and one in diamonds. That's a total of ten tricks, exactly what is required.

West may take the first two club tricks and then lead the ♦K, or lead the ♦K initially. In either case, after winning the ♦A, declarer's priority is to draw trumps since there are enough tricks to make the contract. It will then be safe to take the spade winners.

DECLARER'S PLAN—THE ABC'S

Declarer: South   Contract: 4♥

ASSESS THE SITUATION

Goal	10
Sure Tricks	10
Extra Tricks Needed	0

BROWSE DECLARER'S CHECKLIST
Not applicable

CONSIDER THE ORDER
- Draw trumps first.
- High card from the short side first in spades.

Since the spade suit is unevenly divided between the two hands, declarer starts with the ♠Q, high card from the *short side* first. The ♠3 is then played to dummy's ♠A and ♠K and declarer has ten tricks. On the third round of spades, declarer *discards* a diamond from the South hand.

Conclusion

If declarer tries to take the spade tricks before drawing trumps, West will trump the third round of spades. West can then take a diamond winner to go with the two club tricks to defeat the contract.

3

Takeout Doubles and the Subsequent Auction

Compare these two auctions. East is the dealer. In the first example, East passes. In the second example, East opens 1♦.

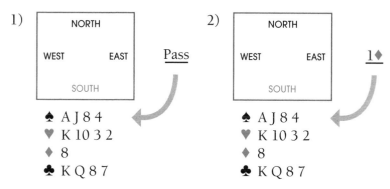

1)

	NORTH	
WEST		EAST
	SOUTH	

Pass

♠ A J 8 4
♥ K 10 3 2
♦ 8
♣ K Q 8 7

2)

	NORTH	
WEST		EAST
	SOUTH	

1♦

♠ A J 8 4
♥ K 10 3 2
♦ 8
♣ K Q 8 7

In the first example, opening 1♣ would be almost unanimous. There are 13 high-card points and no distribution points counting length. The hand is unsuitable for an opening 1NT bid because the hand isn't balanced, and it isn't strong enough. It's not appropriate for a 1♥ or 1♠ opening bid because there is no five-card major suit.

The second hand, the same as the first, has the strength for an overcall when East opens 1♦, but it doesn't have the distribution, which requires a good five-card or longer suit.

Here's the second auction again.

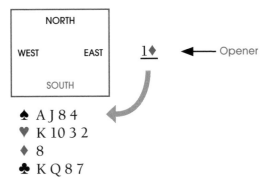

With 13 high-card points, South would have opened if East had passed. That's no longer an option, but South would still like to compete for the privilege of naming the trump suit, preferring any trump suit other than diamonds. Yet the hand doesn't meet the requirements for an overcall since there is no five-card or longer suit.

The *takeout double* can be used to solve this challenge. Since it is rare to double the opponents for penalty at the one level in a trump suit of their choosing, the double is assigned another meaning. It is used to ask partner to choose a trump suit.

Basically, the double sends the message: "I have enough strength to compete for the contract; I'd like you to choose the trump suit." Used in this manner, the double is referred to as a takeout double. Partner is being asked to take the double out into one of the unbid suits, a suit that hasn't been bid by the opponents.

There are risks. By doubling, South gives information about the hand to the opponents as well as partner. This might help declarer make better decisions during the play if East-West win the auction.

Requirements for a Takeout Double

Distribution

The takeout double shows support for whichever suit partner chooses. After all, the doubler is asking partner to pick a suit. Doubler doesn't want to play in a contract where the opponents have more trumps than doubler's side. It would be nice if doubler could always have at least four cards in whichever suit partner chooses. In practice, doubler may have three-card support for one of the possible suits, but it's best not to stray too much further from the ideal unless there is extra strength.

Hand Valuation

If doubler asks partner to pick the suit and wins the auction, doubler's hand will go down on the table as dummy. For this reason, value the distribution using dummy points instead of length points: void – 5; singleton – 3; doubleton – 1.

Strength

The takeout double requires the same values needed to open the bidding, about 12 or more *valuation points*. The high-card valuation points are the same as those used for opening the bidding or responding: Ace – 4; King – 3; Queen – 2; Jack – 1.

The Takeout Double	
DISTRIBUTION:	Support for the unbid suits: At least three-card support, preferably four-card support.
STRENGTH:	12 or more total points, counting high-card points and dummy points: void = 5 singleton = 3 doubleton = 1

Hands Meeting Requirements for a Takeout Double

The following hands meet the requirements for a takeout double by South after East opens 1♦.

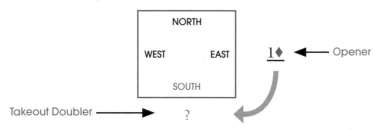

♠ Q 10 8 5
♥ A J 10 7
♦ 5
♣ A Q 6 3

Double. This is the ideal *pattern* for a takeout double, shortness in diamonds, the opponent's suit, and four-card support for each of the unbid suits. South has 13 high-card points and can add 3 dummy points for the singleton diamond, a total of 16 points.

♠ A Q J 5
♥ J 9 6 4
♦ 9 4
♣ A Q 6

Double. This hand qualifies for a takeout double because of the four-card support for hearts and spades and reasonable three-card support if partner chooses clubs. South has 14 high-card points plus 1 dummy point for the doubleton diamond.

♠ Q J 10 3
♥ A 10 9 7
♦ —
♣ K 9 7 5 2

Double. 10 high-card points plus 5 dummy points for the diamond void meets the requirements for a takeout double. With a five-card suit, South might consider making an overcall. However, clubs would have to be bid at the two level and the suit is not very good and the hand is not strong enough. The takeout double is more descriptive than an overcall and gives the partnership the best chance of finding a suitable trump fit.

Hands Not Meeting Requirements for a Takeout Double

The following hands don't meet the requirements for a takeout double by South after East opens 1♦.

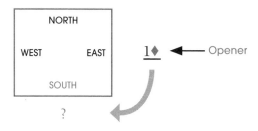

♠ Q 3
♥ K Q 8 5
♦ K J 4 2
♣ Q 7 5

Pass. This hand isn't suitable for an overcall since there is no five-card or longer suit. It is also unsuitable for a takeout double of 1♦. Although South has support for hearts, there isn't support if North chooses spades, and the support isn't that good if North picks clubs.

♠ A K J 8 4
♥ Q 10 3
♦ 6 4
♣ Q 10 8

1♠. On this hand, South has a definite preference for spades and overcalls 1♠. South doesn't want to make a takeout double asking North to choose the suit when spades is the suit South would like to suggest as trumps.

♠ Q 8 7 4
♥ K 10 9 3
♦ 6 4
♣ A 10 8

Pass. South has support for the unbid suits but not enough strength to make a takeout double – 9 high-card points plus 1 dummy point for the doubleton diamond. North would expect a better hand.

The Takeout Double After Both Opponents Have Bid

The takeout double can be used after both opponents have bid[16]. You are still asking partner to pick a trump suit other than the suit(s) suggested by the opponents.

For example, suppose West opens 1♣, North passes, and East responds 1♥.

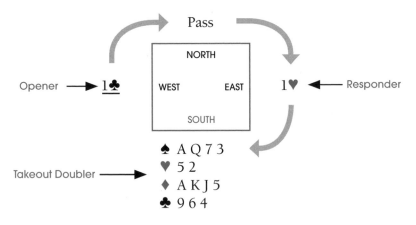

Double. In this auction, there are only two unbid suits, spades and diamonds. South has support for both suits and 14 high-card points plus 1 dummy point for the doubleton heart. By making a takeout double, South is asking North to choose either spades or diamonds as a trump suit.

---

[16] See Practice Deal #32 for an example of a takeout double after both opponents have bid.

Suppose West opens 1♥, North passes, and East raises to 2♥.

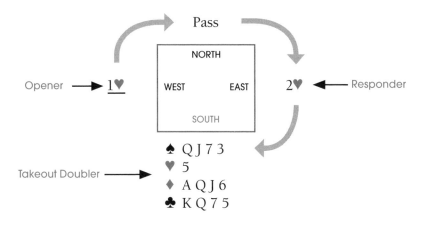

Double. After East raises West's suit, there are still three unbid suits and South has support for all of them. By doubling, the partnership is committed to at least the two level if North chooses spades, or the three level if North chooses a minor suit, either clubs or diamonds. With 15 high-card points plus 3 dummy points for the singleton heart, South has enough strength to get into the auction.

Higher-Level Takeout Doubles

In general, the higher the level at which the takeout double is made, the more strength the doubler requires since the partnership will be committed to taking more tricks[17].

---

[17] See Practice Deals #17 and #29 for examples of takeout doubles at higher levels.

Guidelines for Advancing a Takeout Double

The partner of the opening bidder is referred to as the responder. The partner of a player making an overcall or a takeout double is referred to as the advancer.

West opens 1♥ and North doubles. East, the responder, passes. The auction now comes to advancer.

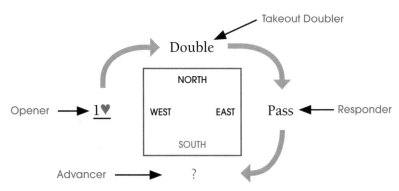

By now, it may not be surprising to hear the requirements for advancing a takeout double are not the same as those for responding to an opening bid or for advancing an overcall. There's a reason for the differences.

First of all, when partner opens the bidding or makes an overcall, partner is suggesting a trump suit and is making an invitation to pass or to bid again. When partner makes a takeout double, advancer is being asked to pick the trump suit. This is more than a request; it's a demand, a forcing bid.

Choosing the Level

Since advancer is not expected to pass, advancer must bid even with no points! There will also be times when advancer wants to bid and explore getting to a game contract. Or, advancer may have the values to bid at a game bonus level opposite partner's takeout double. The guidelines take this into consideration:

Advancing a Takeout Double

- 12+ points Get the partnership to game.
- 9-11 points Make an invitational bid
       by jumping one level.
- 0-8 points Bid at the cheapest level[18].

Choosing the Suit

Partner has asked advancer to choose a trump suit and advancer generally picks the longest suit, since that should be the longest combined suit for the partnership. With a choice between a major suit and a minor suit, the major suit is preferable. Major suit contracts are worth more and fewer tricks are required if you are going for game. As a guideline, with a choice of suits, bid the higher-ranking.

---

[18] Depending on the level of the takeout double and responder's actions, there may not always be room for advancer to jump. This is discussed further in Chapter 4.

Examples with 0-8 points

West opens 1♦, North doubles, and East passes. Advancer has to decide what call to make.

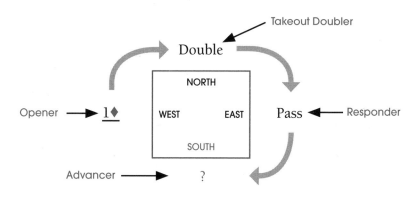

♠ 10 7 6 4 2
♥ 10 8 5
♦ 9 6 3
♣ 8 4

1♠. North asked South to choose a suit and has made a forcing bid. If South passes, West will be left to play in a contract of 1♦ doubled. Diamonds is the opponent's choice of trump suit. North is unlikely to have more than one or two diamonds, and it's only the one level, so declarer is likely to make the contract, probably with overtricks. North is aware South could have no high cards and is merely asking South to give an opinion on the best trump suit for the partnership.

♠ 10 6
♥ J 10 7 6
♦ 9 8 5
♣ A Q 6 2

1♥. Although South's clubs are stronger than the hearts, it's better to show the major suit. South can do so at a lower level and major suit contracts are worth more than minor suits. With two suits of equal length, choose the major suit. With 0–8 points, South bids at the cheapest level.

♠ Q 4
♥ 9 6 3
♦ 10 8 2
♣ Q J 8 6 4

2♣. South bids the longest suit at the cheapest level. Although South is bidding a new suit at the two level, 11 or more points are not needed when advancing a takeout double. Also 2♣ is not forcing. North asked South to bid and the situation is more comparable to raising North's suit than introducing a new suit.

West deals and opens with a weak 2♥ bid. North doubles, and East passes. Advancer has to decide what call to make.

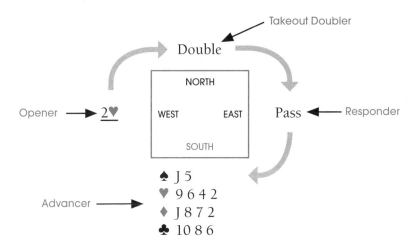

3♦. When North makes a takeout double of West's 2♥ opening bid, the cheapest level available to bid the longest suit is the three level. South isn't promising any strength by advancing to 3♦. North will have taken this possibility into account when choosing to make a takeout double at this level and should have extra strength.

Examples with 9-11 points

West opens 1♥, North doubles, and East passes.

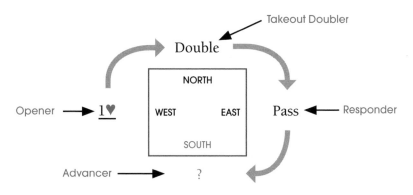

♠ A Q 7 4
♥ 6 3
♦ K J 8 6
♣ 10 9 3

2♠. South would advance to 1♠ with a hand in the 0-8 point range. Here there are 10 high-card points and the partnership is close to the combined strength needed for a game bonus. By jumping a level of the bidding when advancing partner's takeout double, South sends an invitational message. North can pass with the minimum values for a takeout double or bid on to game with a little extra.

♠ K 4
♥ 9 7 2
♦ A Q 10 8 6 3
♣ 6 4

3♦. With 9 high-card points plus 2 length points for the six-card suit, South makes an invitational bid by jumping a level, advancing to 3♦ rather than 2♦. The partnership should be safe at the three level since North is showing an opening bid with support for the suit South chooses. If North has extra strength, a game contract is in sight.

Examples with 12+ points

West opens 1♣, North doubles, and East passes.

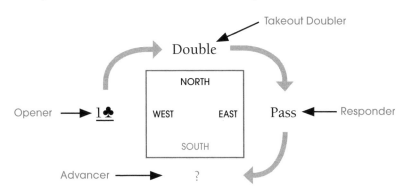

♠ A 8 3
♥ K Q 7 6 5
♦ J 7 6
♣ Q J

4♥. South has 13 high-card points plus 1 length point for the five-card heart suit. South bids to a contract the partnership should be able to make. North has the values for an opening bid with support for hearts. That's enough information to tell South what to do. South knows HOW HIGH, game; South knows WHERE, hearts.

♠ Q J 9 7 5 2
♥ A 2
♦ J 7
♣ K 7 3

4♠. South has 11 high-card points plus 2 length points for the six-card suit. Game in spades looks like the best spot for the partnership.

When Advancer Doesn't Have to Bid

Advancer is expected to bid, even with no points, if the next player passes after the takeout double. Otherwise, the opponents would be left to play in their doubled contract. If advancer's right-hand opponent bids, however, advancer can pass with a weak hand.

West opens 1♥, North doubles, and East raises to 2♥.

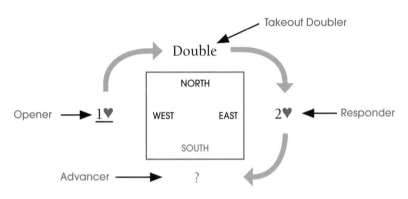

♠ 7 6
♥ J 9 2
♦ J 8 7 5 2
♣ 10 8 4

Pass. If East had passed, South would bid 2♦ to prevent the opponents from playing in 1♥ doubled. When East raises opener's heart suit to 2♥, South is no longer obliged to bid.

Although South doesn't have to bid, South may want to compete after East bids. North's takeout double has promised 12 or more points and shown a desire to compete for the contract. So, with 6 or more points, South should try to bid when possible. For example:

♠ Q 10 7 5
♥ 9 7 3
♦ 10 8
♣ K Q 7 2

2♠. South is no longer forced to bid after East's raise to 2♥ but, with 7 high-card points, South should compete for the contract. North-South likely have as much combined strength as East-West, so they don't want to let East-West choose the trump suit without a struggle. 2♠ is not a jump, so North won't expect any more than 6-8 points.

Advancer Can't Support Doubler's Suits

The takeout doubler has asked advancer to choose an unbid suit as a trump suit. Advancer seldom considers playing in notrump, especially since the takeout doubler is usually short in the opponent's suit. With length and strength in the opponent's suit, however, advancer can consider bidding notrump, using this guideline[19]:

Advancing in Notrump

With strength in the opponent's suit and no better option, bid notrump using the following ranges:

- 13+ points   Bid game in notrump.
- 11-12 points   Bid notrump, jumping a level.
- 6-10 points   Bid notrump at the cheapest level.

---

[19] With 0-5 points, don't bid notrump. Pick an unbid suit, even if it is only three cards.

Here are examples for South after West opens 1♦, North doubles, and East passes.

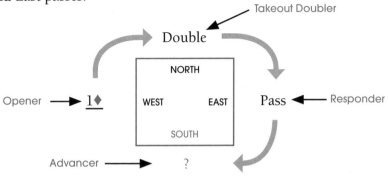

Opener ➔ 1♦

Takeout Doubler

Double

NORTH
WEST   EAST
SOUTH

Pass ◄— Responder

Advancer ➔ ?

♠ Q 8 4
♥ 9 6 3
♦ A J 10 7
♣ J 8 2

1NT. With length and strength in diamonds, the opponent's suit, and 8 high-card points, an advance of 1NT is the best option for South.

♠ J 10 3
♥ Q 10 5
♦ A K J
♣ 9 8 6 3

2NT. With 11 high-card points, South has enough to make a jump response to 3♣. With so much strength in diamonds, however, an advance of 2NT is a better description of the hand.

♠ 9 7 3
♥ Q J 2
♦ K Q 10 8
♣ A J 2

3NT. With 13 high-card points opposite North's takeout double, the partnership belongs in a game contract. With enough length and strength in diamonds, South chooses 3NT.

♠ 10 8 4 2
♥ 6 5
♦ Q 8 6 3
♣ 9 7 2

1♠. Although South's best suit is diamonds, there isn't enough strength to bid 1NT. South simply bids spades at the cheapest level.

Advancer's Forcing Bid

The bid of a new suit by advancer is not forcing and shows 0-8 points. Even a jump by advancer is not forcing, showing an invitational hand of about 9-11 points. With 12 or more points, advancer can jump to a game contract, but advancer sometimes needs more information from the takeout doubler to help decide WHERE the partnership belongs. The only forcing bid available to advancer is the cuebid, the bid of the opponent's suit[20].

For example, suppose West opens 1♦, North doubles, and East passes.

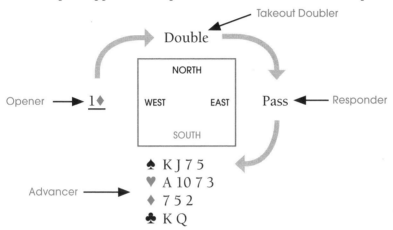

With 13 high-card points opposite North's takeout double, South knows the partnership has enough combined strength for game, but which game? South could guess to jump to 4♥ or 4♠, but the partnership might land in a 4-3 trump fit. Ideally, North will have four-card support for whichever suit South chooses, but North will sometimes have only three-card support.

The solution is to make a forcing call, 2♦, a cuebid of the opponent's suit. Diamonds is the one suit North and South do not want to choose as trumps. After the cuebid of 2♦, North can make a descriptive bid. With a four-card or longer heart suit, North bids 2♥. South now jumps to 4♥, assured the partnership will be in an eight-card fit. With only three hearts, North can bid 2♠ with a four-card suit. South now jumps to 4♠, again assured of landing in the partnership's best fit.

---

[20] See Practice Deal #31 for an example of using the cuebid to reach the best contract.

Rebids by the Takeout Doubler

Doubler Further Describes the Hand

The takeout double promises at least 12 points but could be made on a much stronger hand. The takeout doubler's strength will fall into one of three ranges:

Doubler's Strength Categories	
Maximum	19+ points
Medium	17-18 points
Minimum	12-16 points

Advancer's bid will also fall into one of three ranges:

Advancer's Strength Categories	
Maximum (a jump to game or cuebid)	12+ points
Medium (an invitational jump)	9-11 points
Minimum (a bid at the cheapest level)	0-8 points

After making a takeout double, doubler combines these two pieces of information to decide whether to bid again.

Rebid by Doubler When Advancer Shows a Minimum Hand (0–8)

When advancer bids at the cheapest level, the doubler must be cautious. Advancer was forced to bid and may have no points. So doubler, with a minimum takeout double, passes; with a medium hand, raises one level; with a maximum, makes a jump raise[21].

---

[21] See Practice Deal #21 for an example of doubler's rebid with a maximum-strength hand.

In the following examples, East opens 1♦ and South makes a takeout double. West passes and North advances 1♥. East, the opener, passes and South, the doubler, now has to decide on a rebid.

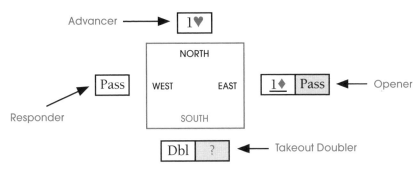

♠ K 10 8 3
♥ A Q 7 5
♦ 7 4
♣ K J 6

Pass. South has 13 high-card points plus 1 dummy point for the doubleton diamond. North has at most 8 points and could have much less. The partnership is high enough.

♠ A Q 7 5
♥ K Q 9 2
♦ 7
♣ K J 8 2

2♥. South has 15 high-card points plus 3 dummy points, a medium-strength hand. North could have 7 or 8 points, so South makes a mild invitation by raising one level. South doesn't bid any higher in case North has a very weak hand.

♠ K Q J 5
♥ A J 7 2
♦ 9 3
♣ A K J

3♥. South has 19 high-card points plus 1 dummy point for the doubleton diamond. Even though South is in the maximum range for a takeout double, South can't afford to take the partnership to game. North may have zero points. Instead, South issues a strong invitation by making a jump raise. North can bid game with 5 or 6 points or more, but can still stop in partscore with a very weak hand.

Rebid by Doubler When Advancer Shows a Medium Hand (9-11)

If advancer makes an invitational bid by jumping a level, doubler accepts the invitation with about 15 or more points. With a bare minimum of 12 to 14 points, doubler passes and stops in partscore.

East opens 1♦ and South doubles. West passes, and North advances with a jump to 2♥. East passes, and South must choose a rebid.

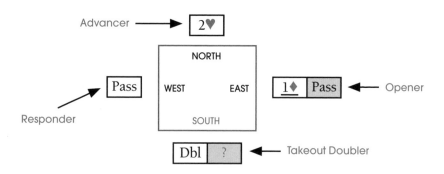

♠ A J 6 2
♥ Q 9 3
♦ 6 5
♣ K Q 9 4

Pass. South has 12 high-card points plus 1 dummy point for the doubleton diamond, a bare minimum. Even if North has 11 points, the partnership does not have the combined strength for game.

♠ K Q 7 3
♥ K J 7 5
♦ 6
♣ A J 5 2

4♥. With 14 high-card points plus 3 dummy point for the singleton diamond, South has more than enough to accept North's invitational bid.

Rebid by Doubler When Advancer Shows a Maximum Hand (12+)

With 12 or more points, advancer will usually have chosen a game contract, so doubler won't have to bid again unless interested in reaching a slam contract. If advancer has made a cuebid, however, doubler must bid again, making a further description of the hand.

East opens 1♦ and South doubles. West passes, and North, advancer, cuebids 2♦. East passes, and South must decide what call to make.

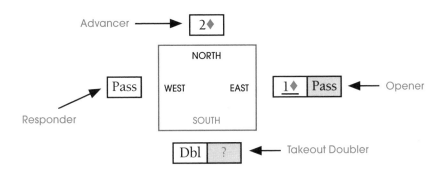

♠ K Q 8 3
♥ A 7 5
♦ 9 8
♣ A 10 9 5

2♠. Advancer's cuebid asks for help in deciding WHERE to play the contract. With a four-card spade suit but only a three-card heart suit, 2♠ is the most descriptive call.

The Double to Show a Strong Overcall

When Doubler has More than 17 Points

The double is a very flexible bid since it takes up no room on the Bidding Ladder. Consider this hand for South after East opens 1♣.

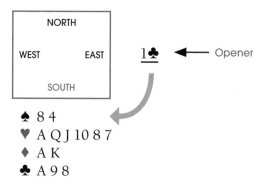

South doesn't have three-card support for either diamonds or spades and, with an excellent six-card heart suit, the hand appears more suitable for an overcall than a takeout double. With 18 high-card points plus 2 length points for the six-card suit, the hand is too strong for an overcall of 1♥. A simple overcall at the one level shows about 7-17 points, so North would not expect such a strong hand. Also, a jump to 2♥ would be preemptive, showing a weak hand, not a strong hand.

To show a hand too strong to overcall, South starts with a double – a forcing bid. North will assume this is a regular takeout double and bid one of the unbid suits, 1♠ for example. At the next opportunity, South bids hearts. This shows a hand too strong for an overcall[22]. North can still pass, but is now aware South holds about 18 or more points. North doesn't need much to move toward a game contract.

---

[22] With an even stronger hand, South doubles first and then jumps in the long suit at the next opportunity or cuebids the opponent's suit.

Here is another example after East opens 1♠.

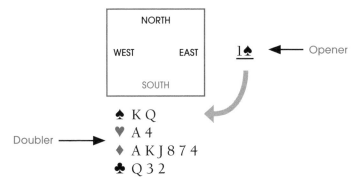

Double. With 19 high-card points and two length points for the six-card diamond suit, South is too strong to overcall 2♦. Instead, South starts with a double. If North bids 2♥, for example, South will next bid 3♦, showing a very strong hand[23].

---

[23] See Practice Deal #25 for an example of using a takeout double to show a strong hand.

Requirements for a Takeout Double

- Distribution: Support for the unbid suits:
                     at least three-card support,
                     preferably four-card support.

- Strength: 12 or more points, counting dummy points:
                     void – 5; singleton – 3; doubleton – 1

Advancing a Takeout Double

- 12+ points: Get the partnership to game.
- 9-11 points: Make an invitational bid by jumping a level.
- 0-8 points: Bid at the cheapest level.

Advancing in Notrump

With strength in the opponent's suit and no better option, bid notrump using the following ranges:

- 13+ points: Bid game in notrump.
- 11-12 points: Bid notrump, jumping a level.
- 6-10 points: Bid notrump at the cheapest level.

Advancer's Forcing Bid

When advancer needs more information to decide How High and Where to play, a cuebid of the opponent's suit is forcing.

Rebids by the Takeout Doubler

The takeout doubler's strength falls approximately into these ranges:

- Maximum: 19+ points.
- Medium: 17-18 points.
- Minimum: 12-16 points.

The takeout doubler combines this with the approximate strength shown by advancer to decide whether to bid again.

Quiz – Part I

East opens 1♥. What call would South make with the following hands?

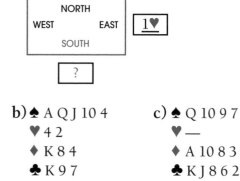

a) ♠ K 10 7 3
   ♥ 7
   ♦ A J 6 2
   ♣ A 9 8 3

b) ♠ A Q J 10 4
   ♥ 4 2
   ♦ K 8 4
   ♣ K 9 7

c) ♠ Q 10 9 7
   ♥ —
   ♦ A 10 8 3
   ♣ K J 8 6 2

d) ♠ Q 8 7
   ♥ 5 3
   ♦ A 9 6 2
   ♣ K 10 7 6

e) ♠ A 10 8 3
   ♥ 9 4
   ♦ Q 9 5
   ♣ A Q 7 4

f) ♠ 9
   ♥ A 9 5 3
   ♦ A J 6 2
   ♣ K J 7 6

West opens the bidding 1♦. North passes and East responds 1♠. What call would South make with each of the following hands?

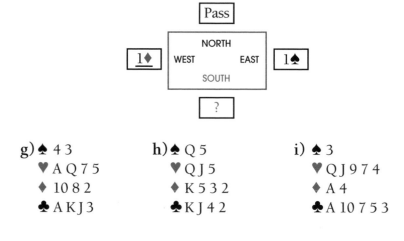

g) ♠ 4 3
   ♥ A Q 7 5
   ♦ 10 8 2
   ♣ A K J 3

h) ♠ Q 5
   ♥ Q J 5
   ♦ K 5 3 2
   ♣ K J 4 2

i) ♠ 3
   ♥ Q J 9 7 4
   ♦ A 4
   ♣ A 10 7 5 3

a) Double. With support for the unbid suits and 12 high-card points plus 3 dummy points for the singleton heart, South makes a takeout double.

b) 1♠. South has the strength and support for a takeout double but, with a clear preference for spades as the trump suit, an overcall of 1♠ is a more descriptive way to enter the auction.

c) Double. Although there are only 10 high-card points, South can add 5 dummy points for the void when considering a takeout double. A double is more effective than an overcall of 2♣ since it gives partner the choice of trump suit and the hand isn't strong enough to overcall 2♣.

d) Pass. South has support for the unbid suits but, with only 9 high-card points, doesn't have enough strength for a takeout double, even adding 1 dummy point for the doubleton heart.

e) Double. With 12 high-card points plus 1 dummy point for the doubleton, South has enough strength for a takeout double. The three-card support for diamonds isn't ideal, but it's good enough.

f) Pass. South has 13 high-card points but doesn't have support for all the unbid suits. If South were to double and North were to choose spades as the trump suit, North-South would be poorly placed. Since South doesn't have a five-card suit, the hand is also unsuitable for an overcall. South passes and awaits developments.

g) Double. When the opponents have bid two suits, South can make a takeout double for the other two suits. South has support for hearts and clubs and, with 14 high-card points plus 1 dummy point for the doubleton spade, enough strength to compete for the contract.

h) Pass. South has 12 high-card points and could add 1 dummy point for the doubleton spade, but South needs to exercise some judgment when deciding whether to make a takeout double. South has only three-card support for hearts and much of the strength is in the opponents' suits. If South doubles, North will have to choose a suit at the two level and the partnership is likely to be much too high.

i) Double. There are only 11 high-card points but South can add three dummy points for the singleton spade and one for the doubleton diamond. That's enough to enter the auction. A takeout double is more flexible than an overcall in one of the suits since it gives partner a choice of two suits.

West opens 1♦. North makes a takeout double and East passes. What call would South make, as advancer, with each of the following hands?

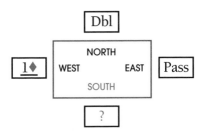

a) ♠ 9 5
♥ 10 7 6 4 2
♦ J 7 3
♣ J 6 4

b) ♠ 8 6 4
♥ Q 7 3
♦ K Q 10 5
♣ A 7 2

c) ♠ K 6 3 2
♥ 8 4
♦ 6 5 3
♣ A 10 8 4

d) ♠ 6 2
♥ A Q 10 4 3
♦ 9 5 4
♣ K 8 4

e) ♠ 9 8 6
♥ K 5
♦ A K J 3
♣ K 7 5 2

f) ♠ A Q 7 5
♥ K Q J 3
♦ 8 3
♣ J 6 2

g) ♠ 8 6 3
♥ 9 5 4
♦ A Q 7 4
♣ J 6 2

h) ♠ 10 3 2
♥ Q 4
♦ 8 7 4
♣ K 8 7 6 5

i) ♠ A K J 7 4 2
♥ Q 3
♦ J 8 4
♣ 6 3

a) 1♥. North has asked South to choose a trump suit and South can't pass if East doesn't bid. South bids the longest suit at the cheapest level.

b) 2NT. Here South has a balanced hand and 11 high-card points, with much of the strength in the opponent's suit. A jump to 2NT is invitational, showing about 11–12 points.

c) 1♠. With a choice of suits to bid, South prefers the major suit. Not only does it keep the auction lower in this situation, if the partnership has enough combined strength for a game contract, game in a major suit requires one less trick than in a minor suit.

d) 2♥. South wants to choose hearts as the trump suit but a bid at the cheapest level would show about 0-8 points. With 9 high-card points plus 1 length point for the five-card suit, South has enough to invite North to bid game with more than a minimum takeout double. South does this by jumping a level to 2♥. Advancer's jump is not forcing, only invitational.

e) 3NT. With 14 high-card points, the partnership has enough combined strength for a game contract. With strength in the opponent's suit, it should be easier to take nine tricks in a notrump contract than eleven tricks in a minor suit game of 5♣.

f) 2♦. The partnership has enough combined strength for a game contract. South has 13 high-card points and North has promised at least 12. The only question is WHERE. North may have four-card support for both hearts and spades but could have only three-card support for one of them. To get more information, South's only forcing bid is a cuebid of the opponent's suit. Over South's 2♦ advance, if North bids 2♥, South can raise to 4♥; if North bids 2♠, South can raise to 4♠.

g) 1NT. With a lot of strength in the opponent's suit and only three cards in each unbid suit, an advance of 1NT is the best choice. This shows about 6-10 points.

h) 2♣. Bidding the long suit at the cheapest level doesn't promise any strength, even at the two level. A new suit by advancer is not forcing.

i) 4♠. South has 11 high-card points plus 2 length points for the six-card suit. Since North is promising at least 12 points with the takeout double, the partnership should have enough combined strength for game. South knows spades will make an excellent trump suit since North promised support for spades. So, South has the information necessary to take the partnership to a game contract of 4♠.

Quiz – Part III

East opens 1♦ and South makes a takeout double. West passes and North, as advancer, bids 1♠, showing about 0-8 points. East passes. What call would South make?

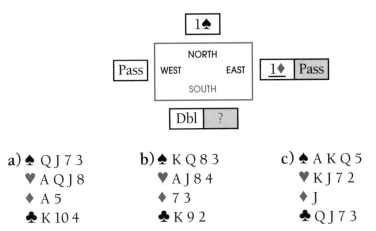

a) ♠ Q J 7 3
♥ A Q J 8
♦ A 5
♣ K 10 4

b) ♠ K Q 8 3
♥ A J 8 4
♦ 7 3
♣ K 9 2

c) ♠ A K Q 5
♥ K J 7 2
♦ J
♣ Q J 7 3

East opens 1♣, South doubles, West passes, and North jumps to 2♥, showing about 9-11 points as advancer. East passes. What call would South make?

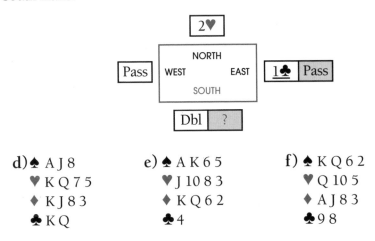

d) ♠ A J 8
♥ K Q 7 5
♦ K J 8 3
♣ K Q

e) ♠ A K 6 5
♥ J 10 8 3
♦ K Q 6 2
♣ 4

f) ♠ K Q 6 2
♥ Q 10 5
♦ A J 8 3
♣ 9 8

Answers to Quiz — Part III

a) 2♠. South has 17 high-card points plus 1 dummy point for the doubleton diamond, a total of 18. If North has 7 or 8 points, the partnership should have enough combined strength for game. South raises to 2♠ to show a medium-strength takeout double. North can pass with a very weak hand of about 0-6 points or move to game with 7 or 8.

b) Pass. With 13 high-card points plus 1 dummy point for the doubleton diamond, South has a minimum-strength hand for the takeout double. North may have no points and has at most about 8. The partnership is high enough.

c) 3♠. South has 17 high-card points plus 3 for the singleton diamond, for a total of 20. With a maximum-strength hand, South makes a highly-invitational jump to 3♠. North can pass with about 0-4 points but continues to game with about 5-8 points.

d) 4♥. South has 19 high-card points plus 1 dummy point for the doubleton club. That's more than enough to accept North's invitation, but not enough to consider bidding any higher.

e) 4♥. South has 13 high-card points plus 3 dummy points for the singleton club. That's enough to accept North's invitational jump to 2♥ and go for the game bonus.

f) Pass. South has 12 high-card points plus 1 point for the doubleton club. With a minimum for the takeout double, South declines North's invitational jump to 2♥. North has about 9-11 points, so partscore should be high enough.

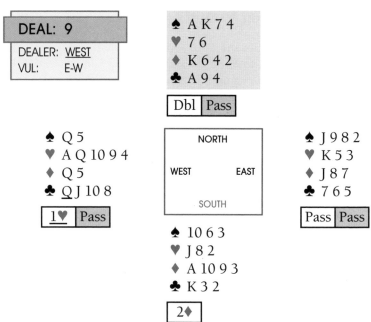

DEAL: 9

DEALER: WEST
VUL: E-W

♠ A K 7 4
♥ 7 6
♦ K 6 4 2
♣ A 9 4

| Dbl | Pass |

♠ Q 5
♥ A Q 10 9 4
♦ Q 5
♣ Q J 10 8

| 1♥ | Pass |

NORTH

WEST   EAST

SOUTH

♠ J 9 8 2
♥ K 5 3
♦ J 8 7
♣ 7 6 5

| Pass | Pass |

♠ 10 6 3
♥ J 8 2
♦ A 10 9 3
♣ K 3 2

| 2♦ |

Suggested Bidding

West is the dealer and opens 1♥. West has 13 high-card points plus 1 length point for the five-card heart suit, enough to open the five-card major at the one level.

North doubles. North would have opened 1♦ if West had passed. After West's 1♥ opening, North can compete by making a takeout double. North has support for the three unbid suits: spades, diamonds, and clubs. North also has 14 high-card points and can add 1 dummy point for the doubleton heart.

East passes. East has only 5 high-card points, not enough to respond.

South advances 2♦. South has 8 high-card points. North has asked South to choose a trump suit other than hearts. South's longest suit is diamonds, so South bids diamonds at the cheapest available level, 2♦.

West passes. West has already described the hand by opening the bidding and passes with nothing extra to show.

North passes. Since South bid diamonds at the cheapest level, South has at most about 8 points and could have zero. North knows the partnership is unlikely to have enough combined strength for game and settles for partscore.

East passes[24], and the auction is over. South is the declarer in 2♦.

Suggested Opening Lead

Against South's 2♦ contract, West leads the ♣Q.

Declarer's Plan

After West leads and dummy comes down, South makes a plan. South's goal is to take at least 8 tricks to make the 2♦ contract. South begins by counting the sure winners: two in spades, two in diamonds, and two in clubs for a total of six. Two more tricks are required.

Moving to the second stage, South browses Declarer's Checklist. The diamond suit offers a chance to develop an extra trick through length. There are eight combined diamonds in the North and South hands. If the missing diamonds divide 3-2, declarer can create an extra

DECLARER'S PLAN—THE ABC'S	
Declarer: South Contract: 2♦	
ASSESS THE SITUATION	
Goal	8
Sure Tricks	6
Extra Tricks Needed	2
BROWSE DECLARER'S CHECKLIST	
Promotion	
Length	1 in diamonds
The Finesse	
Trumping in Dummy	1 in hearts
CONSIDER THE ORDER	
• Draw trumps.	
• Develop the extra diamond trick early.	
• Keep one trump in dummy to ruff a heart.	

winner in that suit. Since declarer has more hearts than dummy, there is also a chance to gain a trick by ruffing one of declarer's hearts with one of dummy's trumps.

After winning the first club trick, declarer draws trumps by playing the ♦A and ♦K. If declarer then leads a third round of diamonds, giving up a trick to East's ♦J, declarer's remaining diamonds are winners.

To ruff a heart in dummy, declarer has to first lose two heart tricks to the defenders. Then dummy will be void in hearts and South's remaining heart can be ruffed with dummy's diamond.

Conclusion

By using the takeout double, North-South find their diamond fit and reach a successful partscore contract despite the opening 1♥ bid. If East-West compete to 2♥, that contract can be defeated by one trick.

---

[24] East might decide to compete to 2♥.

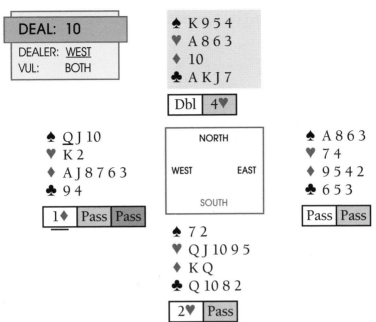

DEAL: 10

DEALER: WEST
VUL: BOTH

North hand:
♠ K 9 5 4
♥ A 8 6 3
♦ 10
♣ A K J 7

Dbl | 4♥

West hand:
♠ Q J 10
♥ K 2
♦ A J 8 7 6 3
♣ 9 4

1♦ | Pass | Pass

East hand:
♠ A 8 6 3
♥ 7 4
♦ 9 5 4 2
♣ 6 5 3

Pass | Pass

NORTH	
WEST	EAST
SOUTH	

South hand:
♠ 7 2
♥ Q J 10 9 5
♦ K Q
♣ Q 10 8 2

2♥ | Pass

Suggested Bidding

West opens 1♦. West has 11 high-card points plus 2 length points for the six-card diamond suit. With enough to open the bidding and no five-card major suit, West starts with the long minor suit, 1♦.

North doubles. With 15 high-card points and support for all of the unbid suits, North would like to compete for the contract. North can add 3 dummy points for the singleton diamond, to bring the total to 18. By making a takeout double, North shows at least the values for an opening bid and asks South to choose the suit.

East passes. East has only 4 high-card points, not enough to respond.

South advances 2♥. Asked to choose a trump suit, South knows WHERE, hearts. South has 10 high-card points plus 1 length point for the five-card heart suit. North has promised at least 12 points, so South jumps to 2♥ to show an invitational hand of about 9-11 points. Since South was forced to bid, an advance to the minimum level of 1♥ would show only 0-8 points.

West passes. West has nothing extra to show.

North raises to 4♥. North has 18 points, more than enough to accept South's invitational jump to 2♥. North knows HOW HIGH, and takes the partnership to game.

Everyone passes, and South is the declarer in 4♥.

Suggested Opening Lead

Against South's 4♥ contract, West would lead the ♠Q.

Declarer's Plan

South's goal is to take at least ten tricks to make the 4♥ contract. South begins by counting the sure winners: one heart and four clubs for a total of five tricks. Five more tricks are required.

South browses Declarer's Checklist. Declarer can promote a diamond winner by driving out the ♦A.

Declarer might hope to get a trick with dummy's ♠K with the help of a finesse if West holds the ♠A. West's opening lead of the ♠Q makes it unlikely this finesse is going to succeed.

Declarer could promote three extra winners in hearts by driving out the ♥K, but that isn't good enough. Instead, declarer must use the concept of the finesse to take all the tricks in hearts without losing a trick to West's ♥K. Declarer does this by leading the ♥Q – or ♥J, ♥10, or ♥9 – from the South hand. If West plays the ♥K, North's ♥A wins and declarer takes the rest of the heart tricks. If West doesn't play the ♥K on South's ♥Q, declarer plays low from dummy and the ♥Q wins. As long as West holds the ♥K, declarer's finesse succeeds. Declarer can repeat the finesse by leading the ♥J if West's ♥K doesn't appear on the first round.

Conclusion

North-South manage to reach a game contract in their best trump suit despite the opening bid by West. North makes use of the takeout double and South cooperates by choosing the suit and showing a hand of invitational strength.

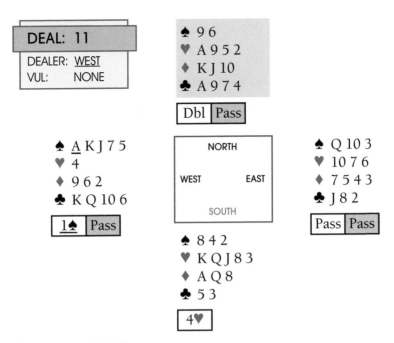

Suggested Bidding

West opens 1♠. West has 13 high-card points plus 1 length point for the five-card spade suit. West opens the five-card major suit.

North doubles. North has only 12 high-card points but can add 1 dummy point for the doubleton spade when considering a takeout double. With 13 points plus support for all three unbid suits, North makes a takeout double.

East passes. East has only 3 high-card points, not enough to respond.

South advances 4♥. South has a definite preference for hearts as the trump suit. So South knows WHERE. In addition, South has 12 high-card points plus 1 length point for the five-card heart suit, for a total of 13. Since North is promising at least opening-bid values for the takeout double, South also knows HOW HIGH. The partnership has enough combined strength for a game contract. Putting this together, South takes the partnership right to a game contract with hearts as trumps, 4♥.

West, North, and East have nothing more to add, so South becomes the declarer in a 4♥ contract.

Suggested Opening Lead

Against South's 4♥ contract, West leads the ♠A, top of the touching high cards. The ♣K, top of the touching high cards in that suit, would also be a reasonable choice.

Declarer's Plan

Declarer makes a plan for playing the hand. South's goal is to take at least ten tricks. South can count on five tricks from the heart suit, three in diamonds, and one in clubs. That's a total of nine tricks. One more is required.

Moving to the second stage, South browses Declarer's Checklist. Since there are more spades in declarer's hand than in dummy, declarer can plan to gain a trick by ruffing the third round of spades in dummy.

Suppose West wins the ♠A and then decides to lead the ♣K to promote a winner in that suit. Declarer wins the ♣A and can start by drawing trumps. It takes three rounds of hearts to draw all the defenders' hearts, but there is still one trump left in dummy. It is then safe for declarer to take the diamond winners. Declarer must be willing to give up a spade trick to the opponents. That leaves declarer in a position to trump the remaining spade with dummy's last heart. The defenders get only two spade tricks and one club trick.

```
DECLARER'S PLAN—THE ABC'S

Declarer: South      Contract: 4♥

ASSESS THE SITUATION
Goal                        10
Sure Tricks                  9
Extra Tricks Needed          1

BROWSE DECLARER'S CHECKLIST
Promotion
Length
The Finesse
Trumping in Dummy    1 in spades

CONSIDER THE ORDER
 • Draw trumps first.
 • Take the losses early.
 • Keep a trump in dummy to ruff a
   spade.
```

Conclusion

North and South are able to reach their game contract in hearts after West's opening bid of 1♠ by effectively using the takeout double. It is important South takes the partnership all the way to the game level. If South made a minimum advance of 2♥, or even an invitational jump to 3♥, North would pass, holding a minimum for the takeout double. The game contract would be missed.

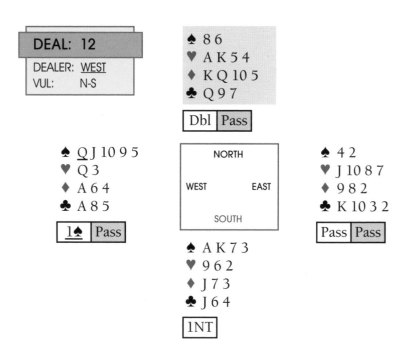

DEAL: 12

DEALER: WEST
VUL: N-S

North hand:
♠ 8 6
♥ A K 5 4
♦ K Q 10 5
♣ Q 9 7

| Dbl | Pass |

West hand:
♠ Q J 10 9 5
♥ Q 3
♦ A 6 4
♣ A 8 5

| 1♠ | Pass |

East hand:
♠ 4 2
♥ J 10 8 7
♦ 9 8 2
♣ K 10 3 2

| Pass | Pass |

South hand:
♠ A K 7 3
♥ 9 6 2
♦ J 7 3
♣ J 6 4

| 1NT |

Suggested Bidding

West deals and opens 1♠. West has 13 high-card points plus 1 length point for the five-card spade suit, enough to open the bidding at the one level in the five-card major.

North doubles. North has support for the unbid suits – hearts, diamonds, and clubs – and can value the hand as 14 high-card points plus 1 dummy point for the doubleton spade. Ideal for a takeout double.

East passes. East, with only 4 high-card points, doesn't have enough to respond.

South advances 1NT. South has 9 high-card points and doesn't have four or more cards in any of the unbid suits. With so much strength in spades, however, South can bid 1NT, suggesting notrump as the best choice of contract for the partnership.

West, North, and East have nothing more to add, so the contract becomes 1NT with South as the declarer.

Suggested Opening Lead

Against South's 1NT contract, West would lead the ♠Q, top of the solid sequence.

Declarer's Plan

South is declarer and the goal is to take seven tricks with no trump suit. South counts two sure tricks in spades and two in hearts. Three more tricks are needed.

South browses Declarer's Checklist. Three tricks can be promoted in diamonds by driving out the ♦A. That's enough to make the contract.

After winning the first spade trick, declarer should go about promoting the extra winners in

```
DECLARER'S PLAN—THE ABC'S

Declarer: South     Contract: 1NT

ASSESS THE SITUATION
Goal                    7
Sure Tricks             4
Extra Tricks Needed     3

BROWSE DECLARER'S CHECKLIST
Promotion           3 in diamonds
Length
The Finesse
Trumping in Dummy

CONSIDER THE ORDER
 • Take the losses early.
```

diamonds, taking the losses early. Declarer can start with the ♦J, high card from the short side, and continue leading diamonds until the defenders take their ♦A. On regaining the lead, declarer can take the established diamond winners to go with the spade and heart winners.

Conclusion

If declarer takes the heart and spade winners before giving up a diamond trick to the defenders, the contract can be defeated. East-West will have eight established winners to take: three spade tricks, two heart tricks, one diamond, and two club tricks.

4

The Competitive Auction

Compare these two examples that seem to have a lot in common.

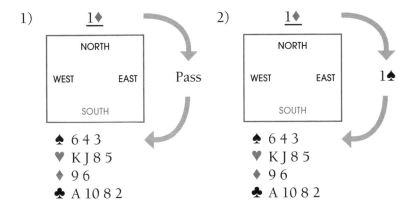

1) 1♦ NORTH WEST EAST SOUTH Pass

♠ 6 4 3
♥ K J 8 5
♦ 9 6
♣ A 10 8 2

2) 1♦ NORTH WEST EAST SOUTH 1♠

♠ 6 4 3
♥ K J 8 5
♦ 9 6
♣ A 10 8 2

In both examples, South has identical hands. North, opens 1♦. The only change between the two hands is East passes in the first example, and overcalls 1♠ in the second. What a difference this makes!

In the first example, after East passes, South can respond 1♥, showing four or more hearts and 6 or more points.

In the second example, East's 1♠ overcall presents a dilemma. South can't respond 1NT because South doesn't have a spade *stopper*. South doesn't have enough strength to bid a new suit at the two level, which would show about 11 or more points. South doesn't want to pass.

Here's the second example again:

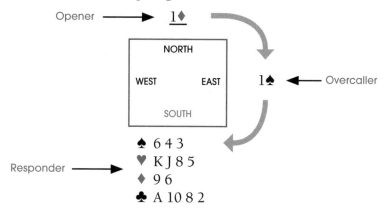

This could be a very uncomfortable auction, but it doesn't have to be.

South can actually be glad East overcalled 1♠. Responder has a tool, and it's best thought of as *responder's double*, because it's only used by responder. It's also known as the *negative double* and it's not for penalty, it's a takeout double. It can solve the dilemma in the second example. Responder, South, can double, showing support for both the unbid suits, hearts and clubs.

If North now bids 2♥ or 2♣, South passes, having found a suitable trump fit. If North doesn't have four cards in hearts or clubs and rebids 1NT or 2♦, South also passes, settling for partscore. More on this shortly.

Responder's Action After an Overcall

All of the players are impacted when the auction is competitive, however, let's start by looking at the impact on responder when right-hand opponent overcalls.

Sometimes, only a minor adjustment is needed; other times, there can be a large impact. Let's consider each scenario in turn.

No Change

North opens the bidding 1♦ and East overcalls 1♥. It's South's call.

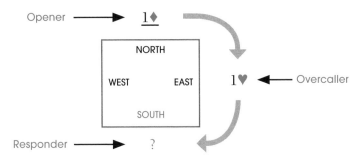

♠ 8 7 5
♥ 10 6 3 2
♦ 8 6
♣ Q J 7 4

Pass. With only 3 high-card points, South was planning to pass North's opening bid. East's 1♥ overcall doesn't affect the decision.

♠ J 8 3
♥ 9 2
♦ K 10 8 6 5
♣ K 6 5

2♦. South was planning to raise partner's diamonds to the two level, showing 6-10 points. The overcall doesn't prevent South from raising to 2♦ to show the diamond support.

♠ J 9 2
♥ A J 10
♦ Q 6 2
♣ J 8 6 5

1NT. If East passed, South would respond 1NT, showing about 6-10 points. South can make the same bid after the 1♥ overcall. However, it's a good idea to have some strength in the overcalled suit when bidding notrump. The opponents will likely lead hearts to try to develop enough tricks to defeat the contract.

♠ K Q 10 7 2
♥ 8 7 3
♦ Q 5
♣ 9 6 5

1♠. South would have responded 1♠ if East had passed. Nothing prevents South from making the same bid. A new suit by responder is still forcing after an overcall and shows 6 or more points at the one level.

Minor Adjustment

North opens the bidding 1♣ and East overcalls 1♠. It's South's call.

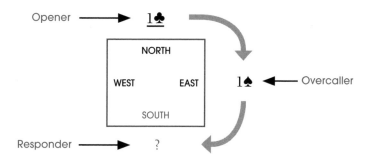

Opener ⟶ 1♣

NORTH

WEST EAST 1♠ ⟵ Overcaller

SOUTH

Responder ⟶ ?

♠ K 10 9 5
♥ 10 7 3
♦ K 10 6
♣ Q 9 2

1NT. South would have responded 1♠, showing 6 or more points and four or more spades, if East had passed. East has taken away that response but 1NT is a reasonable compromise with 8 high-card points and some strength in spades.

♠ 9 8 4
♥ A K J 9 2
♦ K 5
♣ Q 6 5

2♥. South would have responded 1♥ if East passed. That would show four or more hearts and at least 6 points, although South could have a much stronger hand. 1♥ is no longer available after the 1♠ overcall, but South has enough strength to bid a new suit at the two level, showing five or more hearts and about 11 or more points.

Large Impact

North opens the bidding 1♦ and East overcalls 2♣. Let's look at South's decision.

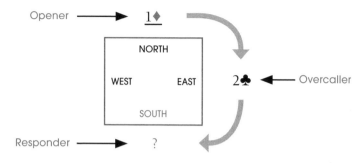

♠ 6 4
♥ K 9 7 5 3
♦ J 6
♣ Q 9 7 2

Pass. South can't bid 2♥ because that would show 11 or more points and would be forcing. The partnership could get too high.

♠ Q 8 6
♥ J 6 3
♦ K 4
♣ J 7 5 3 2

Pass. South would have responded 1NT if East passed. After the 2♣ overcall, South doesn't have enough strength to bid 2NT, which would show an invitational hand of about 11-12 points. Instead, South passes for now. The auction isn't over. North will get another chance to bid and can take some action with extra strength or a suitable hand for competing further. So, it is unlikely North-South will miss a game contract if there is one.

Other Options

The opponent's overcall provides the following extra options for responder:

- Responder's preemptive jump raise
- Responder's cuebid
- Responder's double, the Negative Double

Responder's Preemptive Jump Raise

Preemptive bids are frequently used in competitive auctions because they make it difficult for the opponents to find their best contract. When right-hand opponent overcalls and responder has four-card or longer support for opener's suit but a weak hand of about 6-9 points, preemptive action becomes a priority. Responder can make a preemptive jump raise using the following guideline:

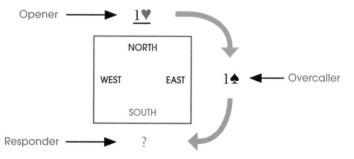

> ### Responder's Preemptive Jump Raise with Support and 6-9 Points[25]
>
> - 4-card support: Jump to the three level.
> - 5-card support: Jump to the game level.

Consider South's call on the following hands where partner opens 1♥ and the next player overcalls 1♠:

Opener ⟶ <u>1♥</u>

```
        NORTH
WEST            EAST       1♠ ⟵ Overcaller
        SOUTH
```

Responder ⟶ ?

♠ 9 3
♥ K J 7 3
♦ J 10 8 7 3
♣ 6 5

3♥. With 5 high-card points plus 1 dummy point for each doubleton, South would raise to 2♥, showing three-card or longer support and 6-9 points if East passed. Once the auction becomes competitive, it is more important to show the fit and also try to keep the opponents out of the auction. A jump to 3♥ is preemptive and it takes away a level of bidding from the opponents.

---

[25] 6-9 points is a guideline. Some players make a preemptive jump raise with fewer than 6 points.

♠ 4
♥ K 10 7 5 3
♦ 6 2
♣ 10 9 7 6 5

4♥. With five-card support and a weak hand, South can make a preemptive raise all the way to the four level. South doesn't expect North to make 4♥, although that's a possibility when South has such excellent trump support and an unbalanced hand with a singleton and doubleton. South expects the opponents can likely make a game unless North has a very good hand. The preemptive jump raise should make it more challenging for East-West to get to their best contract[26].

With only three-card support, responder doesn't make a pre-emptive raise.

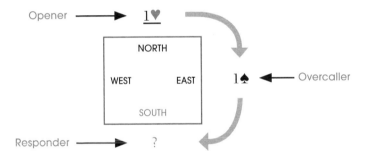

♠ Q 8
♥ A 9 5
♦ 10 7 4 2
♣ Q 8 6 2

2♥. With three-card support for North's suit, South settles for a single raise to the two level. That might be the best spot for North-South and there's no reason to expect the opponents can make a game when South has such a balanced hand with high cards in spades and clubs.

[26] See Practice Deal 22 for an example of responder's preemptive jump raise in action.

Support for Opener's Suit

With three-card support and 11 or more points, responder usually bids a new suit, planning to show the support at the next opportunity.

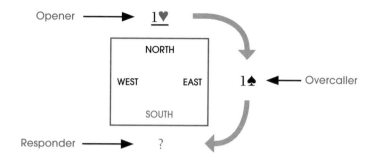

♠ 7 4
♥ Q 9 3
♦ A Q 8 6 5
♣ K 9 2

2♦. With only three-card heart support and 11 or more points, South starts by bidding a new suit, planning to raise hearts at the next opportunity. A cuebid usually promises at least four-card support.

Responder's Cuebid

Responder can use a bid of the opponent's suit, a cuebid, as an artificial forcing bid[27]. The cuebid shows four-card or longer support for opener's suit and at least invitational strength – 11 or more points.

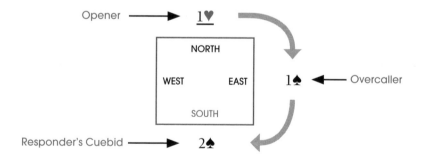

---

[27] Replacing the limit raise with the cuebid is what allows responder to use the jump raise as preemptive after an overcall. See Practice Deal #20 for an example of responder's cuebid in action.

For example, North opens 1♥ and East overcalls 1♠. It's South's call.

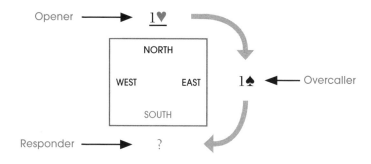

♠ 9 6	**2♠.** With 11 high-card points plus 1 dummy point for the doubleton spade, South would have made a limit raise to 3♥ if East had passed. When East overcalls 1♠, South shows this type of hand with a cuebid of 2♠.
♥ K Q 7 5	
♦ K Q 6 4	
♣ J 4 3	

♠ 8 7 2	**2♠.** With 13 high-card points and four-card heart support, South starts with a cuebid of spades, the opponent's suit. South plans to continue to 4♥ even if opener shows a minimum hand.
♥ A 10 7 3	
♦ K 7 5	
♣ A Q 5	

Subsequent Auction After a Cuebid

When responder cuebids, opener rebids the agreed trump suit at the cheapest level when holding a minimum hand. With more than a minimum, opener jumps to game, accepting the invitation.

If responder has more than an invitational hand for the cuebid, responder will continue to game even if opener rejects the invitation by returning to the agreed suit at the cheapest level.

Responder's Double – The Negative Double

At one time, the double of an opponent's overcall by responder was treated as a *penalty double*. The modern style is to use responder's double for takeout, similar to the takeout double of an opponent's opening bid. Responder's double is referred to as a *negative double*. The term 'negative' means not for penalty.

A double by responder is for takeout when partner opens the bidding at the one level in a suit and the next player overcalls a suit up to and including 4♥[28].

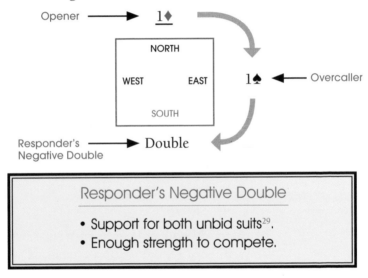

Opener ⟶ 1♦

NORTH

WEST   EAST   1♠ ⟵ Overcaller

SOUTH

Responder's ⟶ Double
Negative Double

Responder's Negative Double

- Support for both unbid suits[29].
- Enough strength to compete.

Support for the Unbid Suits

Since opener has bid one suit and the opponent on responder's right has overcalled in another suit, there will always be two unbid suits. Responder ideally has four-card support for each unbid suit.

---

[28] Some partnerships play negative doubles only through lower levels or through higher levels.

[29] In practice, responder can sometimes get away without support for an unbid minor suit, provided responder has the strength or distribution to bid something else if opener bids the minor.

Strength to Compete

The strength responder needs to make a negative double depends on the level opener will be forced to bid. If there is room for opener to bid one of responder's suits at the one or two level, responder needs only about 6 or more points. If opener may have to bid at the three level, responder needs about 9 or more points. If opener may have to bid at the four level, responder will need about 11 or more points.

Here are examples of hands for responder's double, the negative double. North opens the bidding 1♦, East overcalls 1♠, and it's South's call.

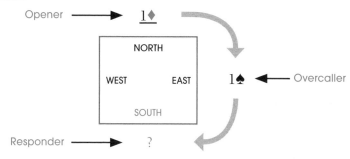

♠ 6 4 3
♥ K J 8 5
♦ 9 6
♣ A 10 8 2

Double. This is the example from the beginning of the chapter. If East hadn't overcalled, South could have responded 1♥, showing four or more hearts and 6 or more points. South doesn't have support for diamonds, or enough strength in spades to bid 1NT, and doesn't have enough strength to bid a new suit at the two level. This is an ideal hand for responder's negative double.

♠ 8 4
♥ A K 6 3
♦ Q 7 4
♣ K J 8 3

Double. Although there is enough strength to bid a new suit at the two level, South can start with the negative double to show support for both unbid suits. With 13 high-card points, South plans to get to game. If North bids 2♥, for example, South will raise to 4♥, putting the partnership in game in the eight-card major suit fit.

Here are examples of hands that are unsuitable for the negative double. North opens 1♥ and East overcalls 2♦.

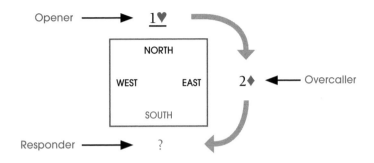

Opener	→	1♥
	NORTH	
WEST	EAST	2♦ ← Overcaller
	SOUTH	
Responder	→	?

♠ Q 9 7 4
♥ 8 6
♦ Q 6 3
♣ J 7 5 2

Pass. South has support for both the unbid suits, spades and clubs but, with only 5 high-card points, there isn't enough strength to compete. If North chooses to bid clubs, for example, it will have to be at the three level and the partnership will be much too high if North has a minimum opening bid.

♠ Q 4
♥ 6 3
♦ 8 7 6 4 2
♣ A Q J 3

Pass. With 9 high-card points, there is enough strength to compete at the two level, but South doesn't have support for both unbid suits. If North were to bid 2♠, the partnership would be in a poor contract.

Responder's Action After a Takeout Double

When right-hand opponent doubles partner's opening bid for takeout, no bidding room is taken up. It would seem responder could make the same call as if there were no double. In practice, the auction has become competitive, so the priority for the partnership has changed. Since right-hand opponent's takeout double has shown the equivalent of an opening bid, there is less chance the partnership is headed for a game contract. The focus shifts to trying to buy the contract or keeping the opponents from reaching their best contract – similar to the situation for responder after an overcall.

Responder's actions are affected because a new call, the *redouble*, is available after a takeout double[30]. A redouble can only be made after an opponent doubles.

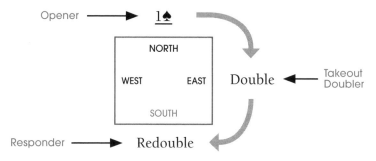

The redouble was originally introduced as a way to increase the score when one side is doubled for penalties. Since a takeout double is not for penalty, however, the redouble can be put to another use.

Responder's Redouble

When partner's opening bid is doubled for takeout, a redouble by responder essentially says, "I think the contract belongs to our side." If the opening bid is in a suit at the one level, use the following guideline when the opponent on your right doubles:

---

[30] Redouble is the last call you need to learn. The only allowable calls in the game are the suit and notrump bids from the one level to the seven level, pass, double, and redouble.

Responder's Redouble

• 10+ high-card points

Here are examples of responder's use of the redouble. North opens the bidding 1♠, East doubles, and it's South's call.

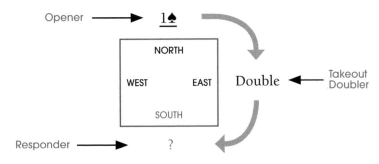

♠ 7 3
♥ K J 9
♦ A J 7 4
♣ J 8 5 3

Redouble. With 10 high-card points, South starts with a redouble. It tells partner the deal belongs to North-South. When the opponents bid, South may choose to double the East-West contract for penalty[31] or continue bidding to North-South's best contract.

♠ Q 2
♥ K 9 4
♦ A K J 7 5 3
♣ 9 5

Redouble. With 13 high-card points plus 2 length points, South would have responded 2♦ if East had passed. The new suit response would be forcing and South would plan to eventually make sure North-South get to at least game. When East doubles, South first redoubles to show 10 or more high-card points. If the opponents now bid 2♣, for example, South plans to bid 2♦ and the partnership can continue bidding as if there had been no interference.

---

[31] See Practice Deal #24 for an example of starting with a redouble and then doubling the opponents' contract for penalty.

136   *Bridge Basics 2 - Competitive Bidding*

Responder's redouble shows about 10 or more points but could be based on a variety of hands. Responder might have a balanced hand, a long suit, or support for opener's suit. As a guideline, opener usually passes the redouble, waiting to see which type of hand responder holds.

The Impact of the Redouble

The impact of having the redouble available is responder's other responses that would typically show about 10 or more points can now be used to show weaker hands. Here are examples of how the availability of the redouble can affect responder's choices. North opens the bidding 1♠ and East doubles for takeout.

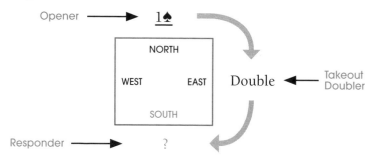

♠ K J 8 5
♥ 3
♦ 8 7 5 3 2
♣ 9 6 2

3♠. With 4 high-card points plus 3 dummy points for the singleton heart, South would raise to only 2♠ if East passed. After the takeout double, a jump raise by responder is preemptive. With enough strength to make a limit raise, showing 11-12 points, South can start with a redouble.

North opens 1♠. East makes a takeout double. It's South's call as responder.

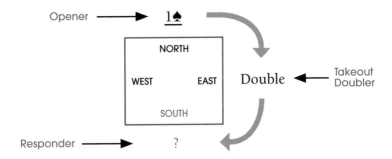

♠ 7 2
♥ 9 4 3
♦ A K J 7 5 3
♣ 9 5

2♦. If East had passed, South would have to respond 1NT because there isn't enough strength to bid a new suit at the two level. After the takeout double, South can afford to respond 2♦. North can draw the inference South has fewer than 10 high-card points because South didn't redouble[32]. A new suit response at the two level is not forcing after a takeout double[33].

Effective use of the redouble requires good cooperation between opener and responder and is a little beyond the scope of this book. It's introduced here to establish it exists and how the meaning of responder's bids are then impacted in a competitive auction.

---

[32] See Practice Deal #23 for an example.

[33] Most partnerships continue to treat a new suit response at the one level as forcing after a takeout double.

Advancing Partner's Overcall After Responder Bids

When an opponent opens the bidding, partner makes an overcall, and responder, the next player, bids or doubles, it won't usually have much effect on advancer's call. Partner's overcall isn't forcing, so advancer doesn't have to bid. However, the overcall has invited advancer into the auction, so advancer should be willing to compete for the auction, usually raising the suit partner overcalled.

West opens the bidding 1♥, North overcalls 1♠, and East bids 2♥. It's South's call as advancer.

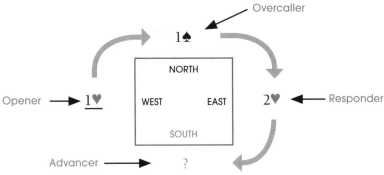

♠ K 10 5
♥ 9 7
♦ K Q 6 4 3
♣ 10 7 5

2♠. With three-card support for partner's suit and 8 high-card points, South would have raised to 2♠ if East had passed. East's 2♥ bid doesn't stop South from making the same call.

A more challenging situation would be if East raised to 3♥ instead of 2♥. Now South can no longer make a comfortable bid of 2♠. South has to decide between passing and making the slight overbid of 3♠. Of course, that is one of the reasons East may have jumped to 3♥ with a weak hand…to present South with a challenge. There's no right answer. Competitive bidding decisions are part of what makes the game so interesting.

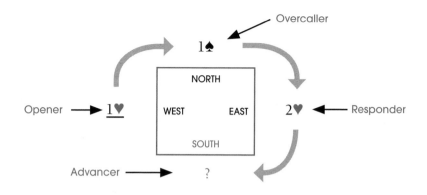

Opener ⟶ 1♥

Overcaller 1♠

Responder ⟶ 2♥

Advancer ⟶ ?

NORTH

WEST   EAST

SOUTH

♠ Q J 7 3
♥ 9
♦ 7 4 2
♣ K 8 6 5 3

3♠. A jump raise of partner's overcall is still preemptive. This is similar to responder's actions in a competitive auction. With enough strength to make an invitational raise of partner's suit, South would make a cuebid of 3♥.

Advancing a Takeout Double if Responder Bids

When partner makes a takeout double, advancer is in a different situation than when partner overcalls. If the opponent on advancer's right passes, advancer is expected to bid something.

Things change when the opponent on advancer's right bids after partner's takeout double. Advancer is no longer forced to bid. However, the takeout double has invited advancer into the auction, so advancer wants to compete whenever possible.

West opens 1♦, North doubles, and East raises to 2♦. It's South's call.

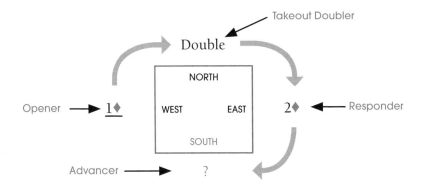

♠ 9 8
♥ 9 7 6 4 2
♦ J 6 5
♣ Q 9 3

Pass. If East had passed, South would have bid 1♥. South can't pass and leave the partnership defending against 1♦ doubled. North wants to play with any suit as trumps except diamonds. Once East bids, South can pass with a weak hand, leaving the contract to East-West unless North bids again.

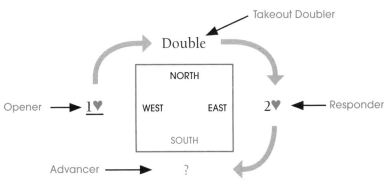

♠ K J 7 4 3
♥ Q 2
♦ 8 6 2
♣ 7 5 2

2♠. If East had passed, South would bid only 1♠ with this hand as advancer. South has only 6 high-card points plus 1 length point for the five-card suit. A jump to 2♠ would be invitational, showing about 9-11 points. When East raises, South doesn't have to bid, but North showed interest in entering the auction and South has enough to compete.

Bidding 2♠ doesn't show too much. With an invitational hand of about 9-11, South could jump to 3♠. With more strength, South could cuebid 3♥, the opponent's suit.

If East were to make a preemptive jump to 3♥, South would probably pass. South doesn't have quite enough to compete at the three level. North would expect a little more. Again, you can see the challenge presented by an opponent's preemptive jump raise.

Action After Making an Overcall or Takeout Double

When an overcall or a takeout double is made, it is usually up to advancer to decide HOW HIGH to compete. However, it may be necessary to act again with extra strength or distribution, or if advancer makes a forcing bid. Here are some examples of South's actions after East opens 1♦.

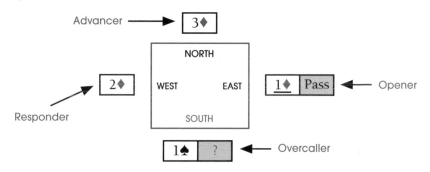

♠ A J 10 9 7 5
♥ A 4
♦ 7 3
♣ K Q 5

4♠. After West raises opener's suit to the two level, North's cuebid shows a hand with at least 11 points. With more than a minimum overcall and a good suit, South can jump to 4♠. With a minimum overcall, South would bid 3♠.

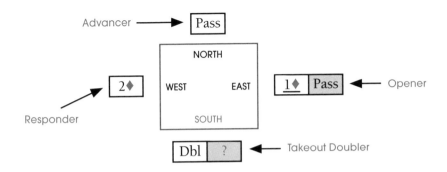

Advancer ——→ Pass

NORTH

WEST   EAST

Responder → 2♦

1♦ Pass ←— Opener

SOUTH

Dbl ? ←— Takeout Doubler

♠ A Q 10 9
♥ A K J 5
♦ 4
♣ K J 9 5

Double. After South's initial takeout double, West raised opener's suit and North passed. North probably doesn't have much. However, South's hand is strong enough to want to compete further. South can make a second takeout double to again ask North to choose a trump suit other than diamonds.

Opener's Action in a Competitive Auction

After the bidding has been opened, the auction can proceed in many ways, especially if the next opponent overcalls. Responder might make a negative double or a cuebid, and opener must choose an appropriate rebid. Opener can also make use of competitive calls such as the double.

Here are some examples of South's rebid in a competitive auction after opening the bidding.

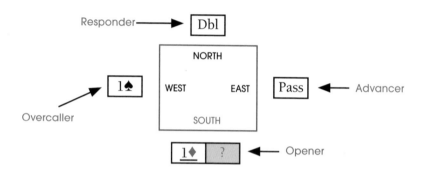

♠ A 8 3
♥ Q 7 5 2
♦ A J 9 8
♣ K 5

2♥. North has made a negative double, showing enough strength to compete and support for the unbid suits, hearts and clubs. With four hearts, South knows there is a fit in hearts. With a minimum opening bid, South bids hearts at the cheapest level, 2♥. In effect, it is as though North responded 1♥ and South raised to 2♥.

With a medium-strength opening bid of about 17-18 points, South would jump to 3♥, inviting North to bid game with more than about 6 or 7 points. With a maximum-strength opening bid of about 19-21 points, South would jump all the way to a game contract.

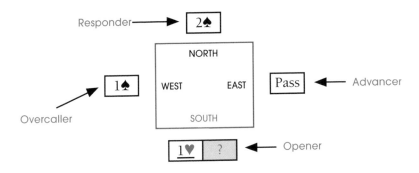

♠ Q 9 7
♥ K J 6 5 2
♦ A 8 3
♣ Q 8

3♥. North's cuebid of the overcalled suit shows support for hearts and a hand with 11 or more points. With a minimum opening bid, South bids 3♥. If South had about 15 or more points, South would jump to game, 4♥. After the 3♥ bid, North will pass with 11-12. With a stronger hand, North will bid again.

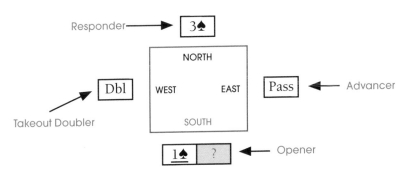

♠ A Q 7 6 3
♥ K 4
♦ K Q 8 5
♣ Q 8

Pass. North's jump raise after the takeout double is preemptive. South has more than a minimum opening bid but, based on North's weakness, South would pass.

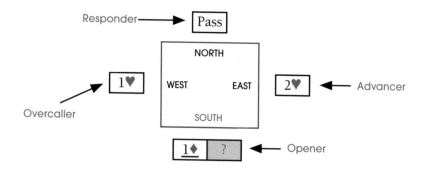

Responder ⟶ Pass

NORTH

WEST   EAST

SOUTH

1♥ ⟵ Overcaller

2♥ ⟵ Advancer

1♦   ? ⟵ Opener

♠ A K 10 8
♥ 6
♦ K Q 8 5
♣ A Q J 6

Double. North passes after South's opening bid and West's overcall. East advances to 2♥. South has enough strength to want to compete for the contract. A double by South at this point is for takeout. South wants North to choose any trump suit other than hearts.

The Penalty Double

Although the double is frequently used to ask partner to bid, it can also be used as a penalty double. A penalty double increases the score for defeating the opponents' contract, and the size of the penalty depends on the opponents' vulnerability.

The penalty double prevents the opponents from frivolously bidding too much. For example, suppose North-South can make a vulnerable game contract of 4♥. At duplicate or *Chicago* bridge, this would be worth 620 points. If East-West were non-vulnerable and the penalty double didn't exist, they could *go down* 10 tricks and only lose 500 points (10 x 50). The penalty double is a deterrent against overbidding. It doesn't stop the opponents from taking a calculated sacrifice against a likely game contract, but it does limit their overbidding.

The downside to doubling for penalty is the opponents will receive an increased score if they make their contract. The trick score will be doubled and they will get a bonus of 50 points for making the contract. There is also a large bonus for making doubled overtricks[34].

It is risky to double the opponents in a partscore contract unless it is certain they can be defeated. If they make their partscore, the trick score is doubled and, if the total is 100 or more points, they now get a game bonus.

---

[34] In addition, the opponents can redouble if they think they can make their contract. That increases the trick score two-fold, but also the penalties if the contract is defeated.

Takeout or Penalty?

Since the double is sometimes used for takeout and sometimes for penalty, the challenge is to know when a double is for takeout and when it is for penalty. A detailed discussion of this topic is outside the scope of this book. For now, a reasonable agreement is:

Distinguishing Penalty Doubles from Takeout Doubles

- Doubles of the opponent's 1NT or 2NT opening bids are for penalty.
- Doubles of the opponents' bids of 4♠ or higher are for penalty.

Here are examples of decisions on whether to double for penalty.

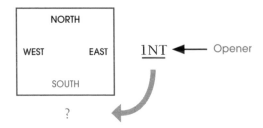

♠ A 9 5
♥ K Q J 10 9
♦ A K 8
♣ K 3

Double. Since there are four unbid suits when the opening bid is 1NT, using a double as takeout isn't very practical. To have support for all four suits, South would need a balanced hand and would be coming into an auction when East has already announced a strong balanced hand of 15-17 points. So, a double of 1NT is commonly treated as a penalty double in standard bidding. On this hand, a penalty double is a better choice than overcalling 2♥. South expects to defeat 1NT by at least one or two tricks after leading the ♥K. The penalty should be more than the score for making a partscore contract of 2♥.

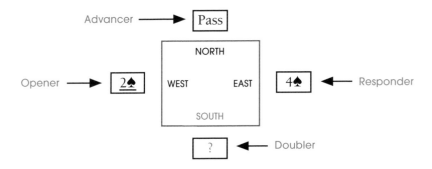

♠ K Q
♥ A K 6
♦ A 10 5 2
♣ A J 7 3

Double. West has opened with a weak two-bid and, based on West's high-card strength, East's jump to 4♠ is likely a preemptive raise, trying to make it difficult for North-South to enter the auction. Since East-West are at the game level, South's double is for penalty. South expects to take at least four or five tricks on defense against 4♠.

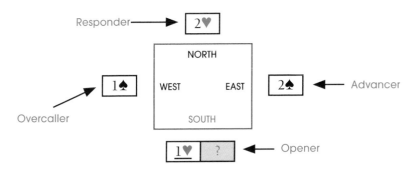

♠ K J 9 5
♥ A Q 8 6 3
♦ 5 2
♣ A 3

Pass. East-West's competitive bidding has prevented North-South from playing in 2♥. South has good defensive prospects against the 2♠ contract but it would be risky to double. There is no guarantee the partnership can take enough tricks to defeat 2♠. If South doubles and East-West make 2♠, they will receive a game bonus instead of the partscore for 2♠.

SUMMARY

Responder's Action After an Overcall

When partner opens the bidding and the next player overcalls, responder can:

- Make the same response that would have been made without the overcall, if that is still possible.
- Make a suitable alternative response if the overcall has impacted responder's original choice.
- Use the new options available after the overcall:
  - Make a preemptive jump raise of opener's suit with four-card or longer support and a weak hand.
  - Use the cuebid of the opponent's suit to show support for opener's suit and at least invitational strength (11+).
  - Use the negative double to show support for the two unbid suits and enough strength to compete.

Responder's Action After a Takeout Double

When partner opens the bidding and the next player makes a takeout double, responder can:

- Redouble with 10 or more high-card points.
- Make a preemptive jump raise of opener's suit with four-card or longer support and a weak hand.
- Bid a new suit at the two level with fewer than 10 points.

Advancer's Actions in a Competitive Auction

When partner has overcalled or made a takeout double, advancer should strive to compete even if responder bids.

Opener's Actions in a Competitive Auction

Opener chooses a rebid based on responder's action. Opener can also use competitive calls such as the double.

The Penalty Double

A double is for penalty if:

- It is a double of an opponent's opening 1NT or 2NT bid.
- It is a double at the 4♠ level or higher.

Quiz – Part I

North opens 1♦ and East overcalls 1♥. What call would South make?

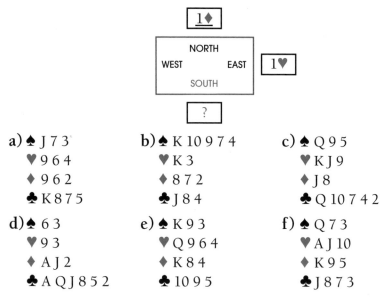

a) ♠ J 7 3
♥ 9 6 4
♦ 9 6 2
♣ K 8 7 5

b) ♠ K 10 9 7 4
♥ K 3
♦ 8 7 2
♣ J 8 4

c) ♠ Q 9 5
♥ K J 9
♦ J 8
♣ Q 10 7 4 2

d) ♠ 6 3
♥ 9 3
♦ A J 2
♣ A Q J 8 5 2

e) ♠ K 9 3
♥ Q 9 6 4
♦ K 8 4
♣ 10 9 5

f) ♠ Q 7 3
♥ A J 10
♦ K 9 5
♣ J 8 7 3

North opens 1♥ and East overcalls 1♠. What call would South make?

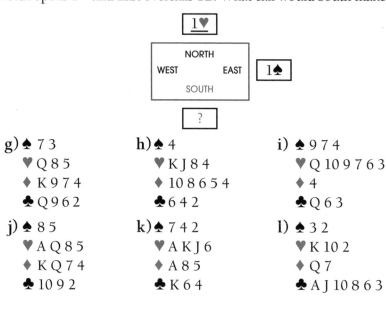

g) ♠ 7 3
♥ Q 8 5
♦ K 9 7 4
♣ Q 9 6 2

h) ♠ 4
♥ K J 8 4
♦ 10 8 6 5 4
♣ 6 4 2

i) ♠ 9 7 4
♥ Q 10 9 7 6 3
♦ 4
♣ Q 6 3

j) ♠ 8 5
♥ A Q 8 5
♦ K Q 7 4
♣ 10 9 2

k) ♠ 7 4 2
♥ A K J 6
♦ A 8 5
♣ K 6 4

l) ♠ 3 2
♥ K 10 2
♦ Q 7
♣ A J 10 8 6 3

a) Pass. With only 4 high-card points, South was planning to pass if East passed. The overcall doesn't change South's decision.

b) 1♠. South would have responded 1♠ if East passed. South can still make the same call.

c) 1NT. With 9 high-card points plus 1 length point for the five-card club suit, South doesn't have enough strength to bid 2♣. Instead, South responds 1NT.

d) 2♣. With 12 high-card points plus 2 length points for the six-card club suit, South has enough to bid a new suit at the two level.

e) 1NT. If East had not overcalled, South would have responded 1♥. After the overcall, 1NT is a reasonable alternative, showing 6-10 points with some strength in hearts.

f) 2NT. A jump to 2NT in response to 1♦ shows a balanced hand with enough strength to invite game, about 11–12 points, and some strength in hearts.

g) 2♥. With three-card support for hearts and 7 high-card points plus 1 dummy point for the doubleton spade, South raises to 2♥.

h) 3♥. With four-card support for hearts and 4 high-card points plus 3 dummy points for the singleton spade, South can make a preemptive jump raise to 3♥ after East's overcall. If East had passed, a jump raise to 3♥ would be invitational, not weak.

i) 4♥. With a weak hand and six-card support for hearts, South can make a preemptive jump raise to 4♥ after the overcall.

j) 2♠. With four-card support and 12 points – 11 high-card points plus 1 dummy point for the doubleton spade – South has enough to cuebid East's spades since a jump raise to 3♥ would be preemptive after the overcall.

k) 2♠. South's cuebid shows four-card or longer heart support and at least 11 points. On this hand, South has enough to continue to 4♥ even if North shows a minimum opening by rebidding 3♥. An immediate jump raise would be preemptive.

l) 2♣. Although South has three-card support for hearts, a cuebid tends to show four-card or longer support. Instead, South starts by bidding a new suit, planning to show the heart support later.

Quiz – Part II

North opens 1♦ and East overcalls 1♠. What call would South make?

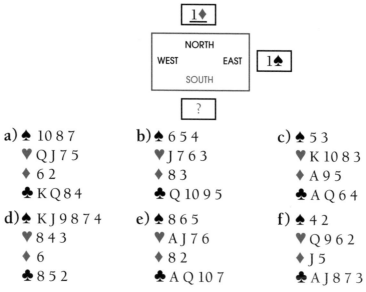

a) ♠ 10 8 7
  ♥ Q J 7 5
  ♦ 6 2
  ♣ K Q 8 4

b) ♠ 6 5 4
  ♥ J 7 6 3
  ♦ 8 3
  ♣ Q 10 9 5

c) ♠ 5 3
  ♥ K 10 8 3
  ♦ A 9 5
  ♣ A Q 6 4

d) ♠ K J 9 8 7 4
  ♥ 8 4 3
  ♦ 6
  ♣ 8 5 2

e) ♠ 8 6 5
  ♥ A J 7 6
  ♦ 8 2
  ♣ A Q 10 7

f) ♠ 4 2
  ♥ Q 9 6 2
  ♦ J 5
  ♣ A J 8 7 3

North opens 1♥ and East doubles. What call would South make?

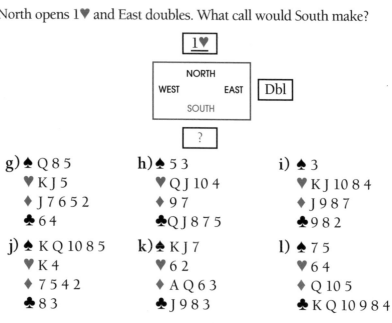

g) ♠ Q 8 5
  ♥ K J 5
  ♦ J 7 6 5 2
  ♣ 6 4

h) ♠ 5 3
  ♥ Q J 10 4
  ♦ 9 7
  ♣ Q J 8 7 5

i) ♠ 3
  ♥ K J 10 8 4
  ♦ J 9 8 7
  ♣ 9 8 2

j) ♠ K Q 10 8 5
  ♥ K 4
  ♦ 7 5 4 2
  ♣ 8 3

k) ♠ K J 7
  ♥ 6 2
  ♦ A Q 6 3
  ♣ J 9 8 3

l) ♠ 7 5
  ♥ 6 4
  ♦ Q 10 5
  ♣ K Q 10 9 8 4

a) Double. If East had passed, South would have responded 1♥. With only 8 high-card points, South isn't strong enough to bid a new suit at the two level but does have enough to compete. With four-card support for both unbid suits, South can make a negative double.

b) Pass. Although South has four-card support for both unbid suits, the hand isn't strong enough to compete for the contract.

c) Double. With 13 high-card points, South has enough to take the partnership to game but starts with a negative double to show support for both unbid suits. If North bids 2♥, for example, South will jump to 4♥ to put the partnership in game in the eight-card fit.

d) Pass. With length and strength in the overcalled suit, South should pass. A double would be negative, for takeout, not for penalty.

e) Double. With support for both unbid suits and 11 high-card points, South starts with a negative double, planning to make a second bid to show a hand of invitational strength.

f) Double. With 8 high-card points plus 1 length point, South has enough to compete by making a negative double after the 1♠ overcall. South isn't strong enough to bid 2♣, a new suit at the two level.

g) 2♥. With 7 high-card points plus 1 dummy point for the doubleton club, South has enough to raise opener's suit to the two level.

h) 3♥. With four-card support for hearts and 6 high-card points plus 1 dummy point for each doubleton, South could raise to 2♥, but a jump raise to 3♥ will likely be more effective in keeping East-West from finding their best contract. After the double, a jump raise is weak.

i) 4♥. With a weak hand and five-card support for North's hearts, South can make a preemptive jump raise to the four level. If North-South can't make 4♥, it's likely East-West can make a contract if left room to find their best spot.

j) 1♠. East's double doesn't prevent South from making the same response South would have made if East had passed.

k) Redouble. With 11 high-card points, South starts with a redouble to tell North the partnership has the majority of the strength.

l) 2♣. After the double, South's 2♣ call is not forcing and shows fewer than 10 high-card points. With 10 or more high-card points, South would start with a redouble.

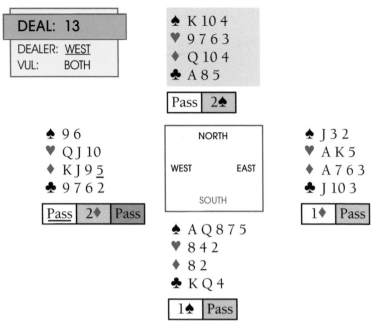

DEAL: 13

DEALER: <u>WEST</u>
VUL: BOTH

♠ K 10 4
♥ 9 7 6 3
♦ Q 10 4
♣ A 8 5

| Pass | 2♠ |

♠ 9 6
♥ Q J 10
♦ K J 9 <u>5</u>
♣ 9 7 6 2

| <u>Pass</u> | 2♦ | Pass |

NORTH

WEST   EAST

SOUTH

♠ J 3 2
♥ A K 5
♦ A 7 6 3
♣ J 10 3

| 1♦ | Pass |

♠ A Q 8 7 5
♥ 8 4 2
♦ 8 2
♣ K Q 4

| 1♠ | Pass |

Suggested Bidding

West is the dealer and passes. West has only 7 high-card points.

North passes. North has only 9 high-card points.

East opens 1♦ in third position. East has 13 high-card points and, with no five-card major, opens the longer minor suit.

South overcalls 1♠. South has 11 high-card points plus 1 length point for the five-card spade suit. With a good suit, South has enough to overcall at the one level.

West raises to 2♦. West has support for opener's minor suit and can compete for the contract by raising to the two level.

North advances 2♠. North also has support for partner's suit and enough strength to compete for the contract. With three-card support and a hand in the minimum range, North competes to the two level.

East passes. East has a minimum opening and nothing further to add to the auction.

South passes. South doesn't have enough strength to bid again since North has shown only about 6-9 points in support of spades.

West also passes, ending the auction. South is the declarer in 2♠.

Suggested Opening Lead

Against South's 2♠ contract, West leads the ♦5, low from three or more cards in the suit bid by the partnership. An alternative would be to lead the ♥Q, top of the solid sequence in hearts.

Declarer's Plan

South's goal is to take at least eight tricks to make the 2♠ contract. South begins by counting the sure winners. There are five in spades if the five missing spades divide 3-2, as might be expected. There are also three in clubs. No more tricks are required.

DECLARER'S PLAN—THE ABC'S	
Declarer: South	Contract: 2♠
ASSESS THE SITUATION	
Goal	8
Sure Tricks	8
Extra Tricks Needed	0
BROWSE DECLARER'S CHECKLIST	
Not applicable	
CONSIDER THE ORDER	
• Draw trumps first.	

The defenders will likely start by taking their two diamond winners and three heart winners. Whatever they lead next, declarer can win the trick. South's priority is to draw the defenders' trumps. This takes three rounds because the five missing spades are divided 3-2.

Once trumps are drawn, it is safe for declarer to take the club winners. On the actual lie, declarer could take the club winners before drawing trumps, but that's a risk declarer doesn't need to take.

Conclusion

On this deal, the overcall doesn't prevent West from raising East's diamonds, the same bid West would have made if South had passed. Similarly, West's raise doesn't prevent North from raising South's overcall. In a competitive auction, both sides try to buy the contract or push the other side too high.

If East-West were to bid 3♦, North-South will still score points by choosing to defend. They can get two spade tricks, one diamond, and three clubs on defense, defeating the contract two tricks. However, if North-South decide to push on to 3♠, now East-West will be the side to receive a positive score since 3♠ can be defeated.

In competitive auctions, both sides must use judgment to decide how to get the biggest plus score, or the smallest minus score.

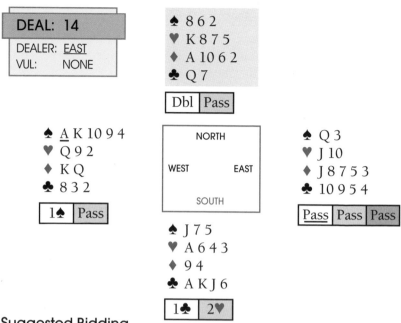

DEAL: 14

DEALER: EAST
VUL: NONE

♠ 8 6 2
♥ K 8 7 5
♦ A 10 6 2
♣ Q 7

| Dbl | Pass |

♠ A K 10 9 4
♥ Q 9 2
♦ K Q
♣ 8 3 2

| 1♠ | Pass |

NORTH

WEST   EAST

SOUTH

♠ Q 3
♥ J 10
♦ J 8 7 5 3
♣ 10 9 5 4

| Pass | Pass | Pass |

♠ J 7 5
♥ A 6 4 3
♦ 9 4
♣ A K J 6

| 1♣ | 2♥ |

Suggested Bidding

East passes. East has only 4 high-card points plus 1 length point for the five-card diamond suit.

South opens 1♣. South has 13 high-card points, enough to open the bidding. With no five-card major suit, South opens the minor suit.

West overcalls 1♠. West has a good five-card suit and more than enough strength to overcall at the one level – 14 high-card points plus 1 length point for the five-card spade suit.

North doubles. North would have responded 1♦ or 1♥ if West had passed but, with only 9 high-card points, doesn't have enough strength to bid a new suit at the two level. A response of 2♥ would show a five-card or longer suit and be forcing, and the partnership might get too high. North does have enough strength to compete, however, and can use responder's double, the negative double, to show support for the unbid suits, hearts and diamonds.

East passes.

South bids 2♥. Since North has shown support for hearts and diamonds, South can put the partnership in its eight-card heart fit.

West passes. West has already described the hand and received no support from partner.

North also passes. South's bid at the cheapest available level has shown no extra strength, so the partnership likely belongs in partscore and has found its heart fit.

East's pass ends the auction, and South is the declarer in 2♥.

Suggested Opening Lead

Against South's 2♥ contract, West would lead the ♠A, top of the touching cards in that suit. The ♦K would be another reasonable choice.

Declarer's Plan

South's goal is to take at least eight tricks to make the 2♥ contract. South begins by counting the sure winners: two hearts, one diamond, and four clubs for a total of seven tricks. One more trick is needed.

Moving to the second stage, South browses Declarer's Checklist. Declarer can develop an extra trick in hearts through length, provided the five missing hearts are divided 3-2.

West may start by leading the ♠A and ♠K, and then a third round which East can trump

DECLARER'S PLAN—THE ABC'S	
Declarer: South	Contract: 2♥
ASSESS THE SITUATION	
Goal	8
Sure Tricks	7
Extra Tricks Needed	1
BROWSE DECLARER'S CHECKLIST	
Promotion	
Length	1 in hearts
The Finesse	
Trumping in Dummy	
CONSIDER THE ORDER	
• Draw trumps first.	
• Play the high card from the short side first in clubs.	

with the ♥10. Whichever suit East now leads, declarer can win. Before taking the club winners, declarer should first draw trumps. Declarer can take two tricks with the ♥A and ♥K and get a third trick in the suit after giving up a trick to West's ♥Q[35].

After regaining the lead, declarer can take the club winners, starting with the ♣Q, high card from the short side first.

Comments

By using the negative double, North and South find the eight-card heart fit despite West's interference. North-South can take eight tricks with hearts as trumps but only seven in a notrump contract.

---

[35] Declarer doesn't have to lead a third round of hearts. Declarer can leave the ♥Q outstanding and take the club winners, letting West win the ♥Q whenever West wants.

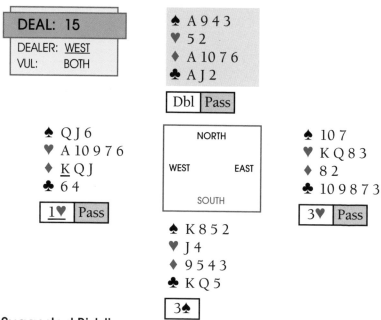

DEAL: 15
DEALER: WEST
VUL: BOTH

NORTH
♠ A 9 4 3
♥ 5 2
♦ A 10 7 6
♣ A J 2

Dbl | Pass

WEST
♠ Q J 6
♥ A 10 9 7 6
♦ K Q J
♣ 6 4

1♥ | Pass

EAST
♠ 10 7
♥ K Q 8 3
♦ 8 2
♣ 10 9 8 7 3

3♥ | Pass

SOUTH
♠ K 8 5 2
♥ J 4
♦ 9 5 4 3
♣ K Q 5

3♠

Suggested Bidding

West deals and opens the bidding 1♥. West has 13 high-card points plus 1 length point for the five-card heart suit. With a balanced hand but not enough strength to open 1NT, West opens the five-card major suit.

North doubles. North has 13 high-card points and can add 1 dummy point for the doubleton heart. With support for the unbid suits, North's hand meets the requirements for a takeout double.

East raises to 3♥. East has 5 high-card points and, with four-card support for opener's suit, can add 1 dummy point for each doubleton. If North had passed, East would raise to only 2♥. North's double, however, has an impact on responder's priorities. With four-card support, East can make a preemptive – weak – jump raise to 3♥ to make it more challenging for North-South to find their best spot. After the double, the jump raise is no longer a limit raise showing about 11-12 points. With that much strength, East could redouble.

South likely bids 3♠. With 9 high-card points, South would bid 2♠ if East passed or raised to 2♥. Over 3♥, South has a challenge. South doesn't want to let East-West win the contract with hearts as trumps, but doesn't have quite enough strength to be comfortable competing to the three level. South will probably make the slight overbid of 3♠.

West passes. West has a minimum opening bid and knows East has a weak hand.

North passes. North also has nothing to add, having already made a takeout double.

East passes. East has done enough, hopefully pushing the opponents too high or causing them to stop too low. East's pass ends the auction and South becomes declarer in 3♠.

Suggested Opening Lead

Against South's 3♠ contract, West leads the ♦K, top of the solid sequence. West might also consider leading the ♥A in the suit bid and raised by the partnership.

Declarer's Plan

South's goal is to take at least nine tricks. South can count on two tricks from the spade suit, one in diamonds, and three in clubs. Three more tricks are required.

DECLARER'S PLAN—THE ABC'S		
Declarer: South	Contract: 3♠	
ASSESS THE SITUATION		
Goal	9	
Sure Tricks	6	
Extra Tricks Needed	3	
BROWSE DECLARER'S CHECKLIST		
Promotion		
Length	1 in spades	
	1 in diamonds	
The Finesse		
Trumping in Dummy		
CONSIDER THE ORDER		
• Draw trumps first.		
• Take the losses early in diamonds.		

With eight combined cards in spades, declarer can plan to gain a trick through length by losing one spade trick. Similarly, declarer can plan to get a trick through length in diamonds. However, in diamonds, declarer will have to lose two tricks.

After winning the ♦A, declarer can start by drawing trumps by taking the ♠A and ♠K. Declarer can leave West's ♠Q outstanding and go to work on diamonds. Declarer gives up a diamond trick to West. If the defenders take their two heart winners and lead a club, declarer wins and gives up one more trick in diamonds. This establishes a diamond trick which can be taken when declarer regains the lead.

Comments

East-West can't make 3♥ since the defenders have two spade losers, a diamond, and two clubs. That's okay since North-South can make 2♠. Even better, the weak jump raise might push North-South too high.

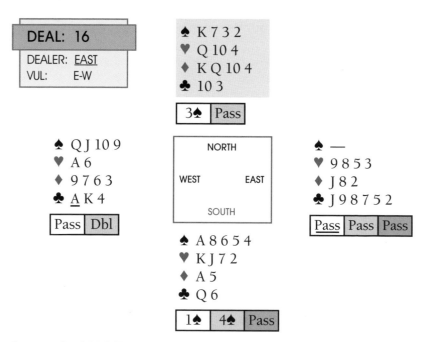

DEAL: 16

DEALER: EAST
VUL: E-W

♠ K 7 3 2
♥ Q 10 4
♦ K Q 10 4
♣ 10 3

| 3♠ | Pass |

♠ Q J 10 9
♥ A 6
♦ 9 7 6 3
♣ A K 4

| Pass | Dbl |

NORTH

WEST   EAST

SOUTH

♠ —
♥ 9 8 5 3
♦ J 8 2
♣ J 9 8 7 5 2

| Pass | Pass | Pass |

♠ A 8 6 5 4
♥ K J 7 2
♦ A 5
♣ Q 6

| 1♠ | 4♠ | Pass |

Suggested Bidding

East deals and passes. East has only 2 high-card points plus 2 length points for the six-card club suit. The club suit isn't suitable for a preemptive opening bid.

South opens 1♠. South has 14 high-card points plus 1 length point for the five-card spade suit. With two doubletons, the hand is unbalanced, so South opens the five-card major suit.

West passes. West has 14 high-card points but doesn't have a five-card suit to overcall and doesn't have support for the unbid suits for a takeout double. With no suitable way to enter the auction, West passes.

North raises to 3♠. North has 10 high-card points and, with four-card support for South's major, can add 1 dummy point for the doubleton club. That's enough to make an invitational jump raise to 3♠.

East passes again.

South bids 4♠. South has more than a minimum opening, enough to accept responder's invitation and continue to game.

West doubles. West is looking at two spade winners after the ♠A and ♠K have been played, the ♥A, and the ♣A-K. West expects to defeat 4♠, likely at least two tricks, and can make a penalty double. West's double is not for takeout. If it were, West would have doubled 1♠.

None of the other players has anything to add, so the contract is 4♠ doubled with South as the declarer.

Suggested Opening Lead

Against South's 4♠ doubled contract, West would lead the ♣A, top of the touching high cards in that suit.

Declarer's Plan

South is declarer and the goal is to take ten tricks. South counts two sure tricks in spades and three in diamonds. Five more tricks need to be developed.

South browses Declarer's Checklist. Three tricks can be promoted in hearts by driving out the ♥A. The spade suit may provide the additional tricks needed through length.

The number of tricks declarer will get from the spade suit depends on how the four missing spades are divided in the defenders' hands. If they are 2-2, declarer can take all the tricks in the spade suit. If they are 3-1, declarer has to lose one trick but will get two tricks through length. If they are 4-0, declarer has to lose two tricks in the suit and will get only one trick through length.

DECLARER'S PLAN—THE ABC'S	
Declarer: South	Contract: 4♠ Dbl
Assess the Situation	
Goal	10
Sure Tricks	5
Extra Tricks Needed	5
Browse Declarer's Checklist	
Promotion	3 in hearts
Length	1-3 in spades
The Finesse	
Trumping in Dummy	
Consider the Order	
• Draw trumps.	
• Take the losses early when promoting winners in the heart suit.	

On the actual deal, the spades divide badly and West gets two tricks in spades to go with the ♥A and ♣A-K. The contract is defeated two tricks. There is nothing declarer can do.

Comments

Even though the contract is defeated by two tricks, there is nothing wrong with the North-South bidding. If the missing trumps were divided 2-2, the game contract would make. The 4-0 division is unlucky.

Additional
Practice Deals

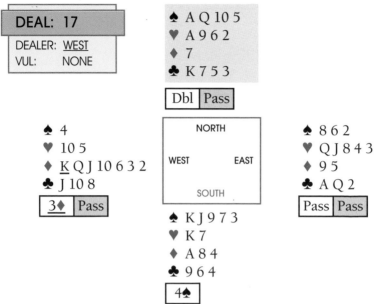

DEAL: 17

DEALER: WEST
VUL: NONE

♠ A Q 10 5
♥ A 9 6 2
♦ 7
♣ K 7 5 3

| Dbl | Pass |

♠ 4
♥ 10 5
♦ K Q J 10 6 3 2
♣ J 10 8

NORTH

WEST   EAST

SOUTH

♠ 8 6 2
♥ Q J 8 4 3
♦ 9 5
♣ A Q 2

| 3♦ | Pass |

| Pass | Pass |

♠ K J 9 7 3
♥ K 7
♦ A 8 4
♣ 9 6 4

| 4♠ |

Suggested Bidding

West is the dealer and opens the bidding 3♦. West has a good seven-card diamond suit and only 7 high-card points, ideal for a preemptive 3♦ opening bid. West's hand is worth six playing tricks with diamonds as trumps.

North doubles. North has a good hand for a takeout double even though the auction is at the three level. North has support for the unbid suits: spades, hearts, and clubs. There are 13 high-card points and 3 dummy points can be added for the singleton diamond, a total of 16 points.

East passes. East has 9 high-card points plus 1 length point for the five-card heart suit but that's not enough to consider game and, with only a doubleton diamond, not enough to compete further by raising West's preemptive bid.

South advances 4♠. South has 11 high-card points plus 1 length point for the five-card spade suit. North has promised at least an opening bid – and likely a bit more to double at the three level – so South knows How High the partnership belongs, game. South also knows Where the partnership belongs, spades. Putting it together, South jumps to 4♠.

West, North, and East pass. South becomes the declarer in 4♠.

Suggested Opening Lead

Against South's 4♠ contract, West will lead the ♦K, top of the solid sequence.

Suggested Play

South's goal is to take ten tricks with spades as the trump suit. There are five sure spade tricks, two heart tricks, and the ♦A. That's a total of eight tricks; two more tricks must be developed.

South browses Declarer's Checklist. One possibility is the finesse in clubs. South could lead toward dummy's ♣K, hoping West holds the ♣A. This is unlikely to work since West's opening bid showed few, if any, high cards outside diamonds. It is more likely

```
DECLARER'S PLAN—THE ABC'S

Declarer: South     Contract: 4♠

ASSESS THE SITUATION
Goal                    10
Sure Tricks              8
Extra Tricks Needed      2

BROWSE DECLARER'S CHECKLIST
Promotion
Length
The Finesse          1 in clubs?
Trumping in Dummy    2 in diamonds

CONSIDER THE ORDER
• Keep enough trumps in the
  dummy to trump two diamonds.
```

East holds the ♣A. There is a second possibility. Since South has more diamonds than dummy, there is an opportnity to trump two diamonds in dummy.

In Considering the Order, declarer needs at least two spades in the dummy to trump diamonds. After winning the ♦A, declarer's best plan is to immediately lead another diamond and trump with North's ♠10[36]. Declarer then takes dummy's ♠A and plays the ♠5 to the ♠K. South leads the remaining diamond and trumps with dummy's ♠Q. Now declarer can lead a low heart from dummy to the ♥K and lead the ♠J to draw East's last trump. Declarer loses only three club tricks.

Conclusion

West's 3♦ opening bid carried little risk. On the lie of the cards, 3♦ can't be defeated since West can promote six diamond winners and take three club tricks with the help of finesses in clubs. The value of the preemptive bid is that it might keep North-South from reaching their 4♠ contract.

---

[36] Declarer trumps with a high spade so East cannot overtrump with a higher spade if East has no diamonds remaining.

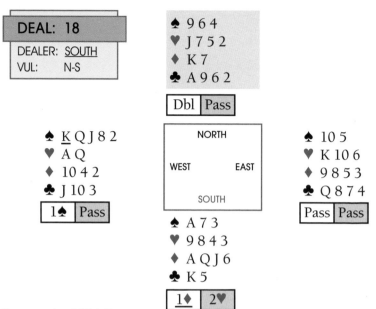

DEAL: 18

DEALER: SOUTH
VUL: N-S

♠ 9 6 4
♥ J 7 5 2
♦ K 7
♣ A 9 6 2

| Dbl | Pass |

NORTH

WEST   EAST

SOUTH

♠ K Q J 8 2
♥ A Q
♦ 10 4 2
♣ J 10 3

| 1♠ | Pass |

♠ 10 5
♥ K 10 6
♦ 9 8 5 3
♣ Q 8 7 4

| Pass | Pass |

♠ A 7 3
♥ 9 8 4 3
♦ A Q J 6
♣ K 5

| 1♦ | 2♥ |

Suggested Bidding

South deals and opens 1♦. South has a balanced hand with 14 high-card points. With no five-card major suit and not enough strength to open 1NT, South opens the longer minor.

West overcalls 1♠. With 13 high-card points plus 1 length point for the five-card spade suit, West can compete for the contract with an overcall.

North doubles. As responder, North would have bid 1♥ if West had passed. After the 1♠ overcall, North doesn't have enough strength to bid a new suit at the two level. With 8 high-card points and support for both unbid suits, hearts and clubs, North does have enough strength to want to compete for the contract. North can use responder's double – the negative double – to describe the hand.

East passes. East is advancer but doesn't have support for spades and only 5 high-card points.

South bids 2♥. South has to choose a rebid after responder's negative double, which is for takeout. With four hearts, even though they are all low cards, South bids 2♥ since North has shown support for hearts.

West, North, and East have nothing further to say and all pass. South becomes the declarer in 2♥.

Suggested Opening Lead

Against South's 2♥ contract, West would lead the ♠K, top of the solid sequence.

Suggested Play

South's goal is to take at least eight tricks. There is one sure spade trick, four diamond tricks, and two club tricks. One more trick is required.

South browses Declarer's Checklist. Even though the ♥A, ♥K, and ♥Q are missing, it may be possible to develop a heart trick through length with eight hearts between the combined hands. South has to hope the five missing hearts are divided 3-2.

Leading hearts also serves the purpose of drawing trumps.

DECLARER'S PLAN—THE ABC'S	
Declarer: South Contract: 4♥	
ASSESS THE SITUATION	
Goal	8
Sure Tricks	7
Extra Tricks Needed	1
BROWSE DECLARER'S CHECKLIST	
Promotion	
Length	1 in hearts
The Finesse	
Trumping in Dummy	
CONSIDER THE ORDER	
• Draw trumps.	
• Develop the extra heart trick early	
• High card from the short side first in diamonds.	

After winning the ♠A, declarer can immediately lead a heart to work on developing the extra trick early[37]. West can win the ♥Q and take two established spade winners, but no more. If West leads a diamond or a club, declarer can win and lead a second round of hearts. West can win the ♥A but, whatever West leads next, declarer can win and lead a third round of hearts to establish a winner after East takes the ♥K[38]. The defenders get only two spade tricks and three heart tricks.

When taking the diamonds, declarer starts with the ♦K, high card from the short side, and then plays the ♦7 over to the ♦A-Q-J.

Conclusion

North and South do well to find their 2♥ contract after West's 1♠ overcall by using the negative double. If East and West bid to 2♠, North-South can defeat that contract at least one trick.

---

[37] On this deal, declarer can actually do better by taking diamond winners early to discard spades from dummy, but drawing trumps works out well enough.

[38] Declarer doesn't have to lead a third round of hearts. Declarer can start taking winners in diamonds and clubs, letting East take a trick with the ♥K whenever East wants.

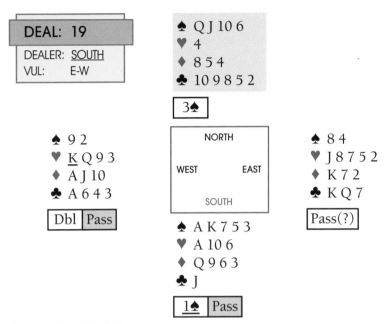

DEAL: 19

DEALER: SOUTH
VUL: E-W

♠ Q J 10 6
♥ 4
♦ 8 5 4
♣ 10 9 8 5 2

3♠

NORTH

WEST   EAST

SOUTH

♠ 9 2
♥ K Q 9 3
♦ A J 10
♣ A 6 4 3

Dbl | Pass

♠ 8 4
♥ J 8 7 5 2
♦ K 7 2
♣ K Q 7

Pass(?)

♠ A K 7 5 3
♥ A 10 6
♦ Q 9 6 3
♣ J

1♠ | Pass

Suggested Bidding

South deals and opens 1♠. South values the hand as 15 points: 14 high-card points plus 1 length point for the five-card spade suit. With an unbalanced hand and a five-card major suit, South opens 1♠.

West doubles. With support for all three unbid suits and 14 high-card points plus 1 dummy point for the doubleton spade, West can make a takeout double.

North jumps to 3♠. North has only 3 high-card points but, with four-card support for South's spades, can add 3 dummy points for the singleton heart, for a total of 6 points. If West had passed, North would raise to only 2♠ but, with an unbalanced hand and all the high-card points in partner's suit, North can make a preemptive raise to 3♠ over West's double. After the double, the jump raise is weak, not a limit raise.

East probably passes. As advancer, East has 9 high-card points plus 1 length point for the five-card heart suit. If North had raised to 2♠, East has enough to compete to 3♥. When North jumps to 3♠, East doesn't have quite enough strength to bid 4♥.

South and West both pass. South is the declarer in 3♠.

Suggested Opening Lead

Against South's 3♠ contract, West would lead the ♥K, top of the touching cards in an unbid suit.

Suggested Play

South's goal is to take nine tricks. There are five spade winners and the ♥A. Three more tricks are needed.

With two more hearts in declarer's hand than dummy, there is the opportunity to gain two tricks by trumping hearts in the dummy. With seven diamonds between the two hands, there is also the possibility to develop a diamond trick through length. This requires the missing diamonds to divide 3-3 which is a little against the odds, but a possibility[39].

DECLARER'S PLAN—THE ABC'S	
Declarer: South Contract: 3♠	
ASSESS THE SITUATION	
Goal	9
Sure Tricks	6
Extra Tricks Needed	3
BROWSE DECLARER'S CHECKLIST	
Promotion	
Length	1 in diamonds
The Finesse	
Trumping in Dummy	2 in hearts
CONSIDER THE ORDER	
• Keep enough trumps in the dummy to trump two hearts.	
• Develop the extra diamond trick early.	

In Considering the Order, declarer must make sure to leave two trumps in dummy to ruff the hearts. Also, declarer should plan to lead diamonds early, before taking all the trump winners.

After winning the ♥A, declarer can lead the ♥6 and trump with one of dummy's spades. Declarer could then lead a diamond, planning to lose a trick in that suit. The defenders can take three diamond tricks and the ♣A, but declarer can eventually trump the ♥10 in dummy, draw trumps, and establish a diamond winner.

Conclusion

North's jump to 3♠ may keep East-West from competing any further. If East-West compete to 4♥, North-South can defeat that contract[40].

---

[39] Declarer could hope to get a trick with the ♦Q by leading twice toward it, hoping East holds both the ♦A and ♦K. That's unlikely since West probably holds at least one high diamond for the takeout double. Another possibility is to try to trump the fourth round of diamonds in the dummy. That's unnecessary on the actual lie of the cards.

[40] If, for example, North leads the ♠Q against 4♥, South can overtake with the ♠K to win the trick and then lead the singleton ♣J. After winning a trick with the ♥A, South can lead a low spade to North's ♠J and North can lead a club for South to trump.

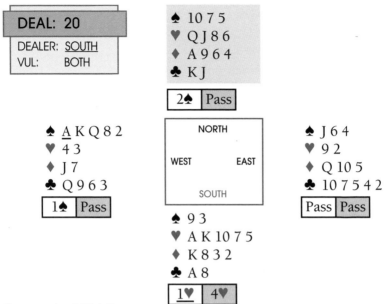

DEAL: 20

DEALER: SOUTH
VUL: BOTH

♠ 10 7 5
♥ Q J 8 6
♦ A 9 6 4
♣ K J

| 2♠ | Pass |

♠ A K Q 8 2
♥ 4 3
♦ J 7
♣ Q 9 6 3

| 1♠ | Pass |

NORTH

WEST   EAST

SOUTH

♠ J 6 4
♥ 9 2
♦ Q 10 5
♣ 10 7 5 4 2

| Pass | Pass |

♠ 9 3
♥ A K 10 7 5
♦ K 8 3 2
♣ A 8

| 1♥ | 4♥ |

Suggested Bidding

South opens 1♥ as dealer. South has 14 high-card points plus 1 length point for the five-card heart suit. With an unbalanced hand, South opens the five-card major suit.

West overcalls 1♠. West has 12 high-card points plus 1 length point for the five-card spade suit. With a good five-card suit, West has more than enough to overcall at the one level.

North bids 2♠. With 11 high-card points and four-card support for South's hearts, North can add 1 dummy point for the doubleton club. If West had passed, North would make a limit raise of 3♥, showing an invitational hand with about 11-12 points. After West's overcall, a jump to 3♥ would be preemptive, not a limit raise. To show the support and about 11 or more points, North cuebids 2♠, West's suit.

East passes. East has three-card support for spades but not enough strength to compete in the auction.

South bids 4♥. South has 15 points. That's enough to take the partnership to game after North cuebids to show support for hearts and 11 or more points.

West, North, and East all pass, ending the auction. South is the declarer in 4♥.

Suggested Opening Lead

Against South's 4♥ contract, West would lead the ♠A, top of the solid sequence.

Suggested Play

The North hand comes down as dummy and South makes a plan. South's goal is to take ten tricks.

South counts the sure tricks. There are five heart tricks, two diamonds, and two club tricks. One more trick is required.

South browses Declarer's Checklist. The diamond suit provides the opportunity for an extra trick through length. There are eight diamonds in the combined hands. If the five missing diamonds are divided 3-2, declarer can keep playing the suit until the defenders have no diamonds left. This establishes a third trick in the suit.

DECLARER'S PLAN—THE ABC'S	
Declarer: South	Contract: 4♥
ASSESS THE SITUATION	
Goal	10
Sure Tricks	9
Extra Tricks Needed	1
BROWSE DECLARER'S CHECKLIST	
Promotion	
Length	1 in diamonds
The Finesse	
Trumping in Dummy	
CONSIDER THE ORDER	
• Draw trumps first.	
• Develop the extra diamond trick early.	

West will likely continue with the ♠K and ♠Q after winning the first trick with the ♠A. South can trump the third round of spades and then draw the defenders' trumps by playing the ♥A and ♥K. Declarer then takes two tricks with the ♦A and ♦K and plays a third round of diamonds, giving up a trick to the defenders. Declarer gives up the diamond trick early, while retaining winners in the other suits with which to regain the lead.

Conclusion

North and South reach their 4♥ contract despite West's 1♠ overcall. If North had jumped to 3♥ after the 1♠ overcall, South would pass, expecting North to hold a weak hand. When North cuebids 2♠, South jumps to 4♥ with some extra strength. If South rebids only 3♥, North might pass, assuming South held a minimum opening bid.

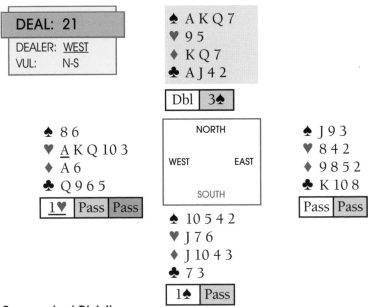

DEAL: 21
DEALER: WEST
VUL: N-S

♠ A K Q 7
♥ 9 5
♦ K Q 7
♣ A J 4 2

| Dbl | 3♠ |

NORTH

WEST   EAST

SOUTH

♠ 8 6
♥ A K Q 10 3
♦ A 6
♣ Q 9 6 5

| 1♥ | Pass | Pass |

♠ J 9 3
♥ 8 4 2
♦ 9 8 5 2
♣ K 10 8

| Pass | Pass |

♠ 10 5 4 2
♥ J 7 6
♦ J 10 4 3
♣ 7 3

| 1♠ | Pass |

Suggested Bidding

West opens 1♥. West has 15 high-card points plus 1 length point for the five-card heart suit. The hand falls in the range for opening 1NT but, with two doubletons, the hand isn't really balanced, so West opens the five-card major suit.

North doubles. North has 19 high-card points plus 1 dummy point for the doubleton heart. With support for all three unbid suits, North makes a takeout double.

East passes with only 4 high-card points.

South advances 1♠. South has only 2 high-card points but, as advancer, can't pass North's takeout double when East passes. South bids the four-card major suit at the one level, showing about 0-8 points.

West passes. West doesn't have much extra for the opening bid and responder hasn't shown any strength. Alternatively, West might choose to show a second suit by bidding 2♣.

North raises to 3♠. North has 20 points and excellent support for spades, but that isn't enough strength to commit the partnership to game. South has been forced to bid and might have no points at all. North issues a strong invitation by jumping to 3♠, showing about 19-21 points.

East, South, and West all pass. South is the declarer in 3♠.

Suggested Opening Lead

West leads the ♥A, top of the solid sequence, against South's 3♠.

Suggested Play

South's goal is to take nine tricks with spades as the trump suit. There are three sure spade tricks and one sure club trick. Five more tricks are needed.

Declarer browses the checklist. If the five missing spades are divided 3-2, as might be expected, the spade suit will provide an extra trick through length. Since declarer has one more heart than dummy, declarer can gain a trick by trumping a heart in dummy. In diamonds, three tricks can be developed through promotion by driving out the ♦A.

DECLARER'S PLAN—THE ABC'S		
Declarer: South	Contract: 3♠	
ASSESS THE SITUATION		
Goal	9	
Sure Tricks	4	
Extra Tricks Needed	5	
BROWSE DECLARER'S CHECKLIST		
Promotion	3 in diamonds	
Length	1 in spades	
The Finesse		
Trumping in Dummy	1 in hearts	
CONSIDER THE ORDER		
• Keep enough trumps in the dummy to trump one heart.		
• Draw trumps.		
• High card from the short side whjen promoting diamond winners.		

That's a lot of work to do, so declarer Considers the Order. Declarer wants to draw trumps before taking any promoted diamond winners. Declarer also wants to keep a spade in dummy to trump a heart.

Suppose West takes the ♥A and ♥K and leads a club. Declarer wins the ♣A and draws the defenders' trumps with the ♠A-K-Q. Now declarer can lead the ♦K, high card from the short side. West can win the ♦A and the defenders can take a club trick, but that's all. If they lead another club, South trumps. South can trump a heart in dummy and take the ♦Q and two more tricks with the ♦J-10.

Conclusion

Despite holding 20 points, North must not take the partnership too high. All North-South can make is a partscore contract in spades. South's 1♠ advance is not the same as a 1♠ response to an opening bid, showing 6 or more points.

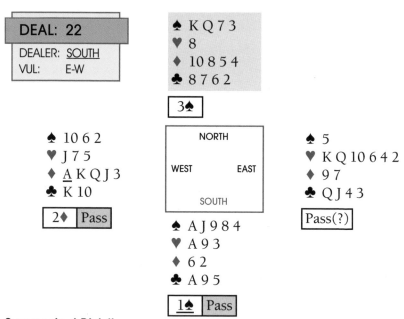

DEAL: 22

DEALER: SOUTH
VUL: E-W

NORTH
♠ K Q 7 3
♥ 8
♦ 10 8 5 4
♣ 8 7 6 2

3♠

WEST
♠ 10 6 2
♥ J 7 5
♦ A K Q J 3
♣ K 10

2♦ | Pass

EAST
♠ 5
♥ K Q 10 6 4 2
♦ 9 7
♣ Q J 4 3

Pass(?)

SOUTH
♠ A J 9 8 4
♥ A 9 3
♦ 6 2
♣ A 9 5

1♠ | Pass

Suggested Bidding

South is the dealer and opens the bidding 1♠. South has 13 high-card points plus 1 length point for the five-card spade suit. South opens the five-card major at the one level.

West overcalls 2♦. West has 14 high-card points and 1 length point for the five-card diamond suit. With a good diamond suit, West has enough to overcall at the two level.

North jumps to 3♠. North has 5 high-card points but, with four-card support for South's spades, can add 3 dummy points for the singleton heart. If West had passed, North would raise to 2♠, showing 6-9 points. Once the auction becomes competitive, taking bidding room away from the opponents becomes important. With four-card support, an unbalanced hand, and a concentration of high cards in spades, North makes a preemptive jump raise to 3♠.

East may pass. As advancer, East might have bid 2♥ if North had passed, and might even compete with 3♥ if North raised to only 2♠. After North raises to 3♠, East will likely keep out of the auction and pass.

South passes. North's jump to 3♠ has not promised much strength.

West passes, and South becomes the declarer in a partscore 3♠ contract.

Suggested Opening Lead

Against South's 3♠ contract, West will lead the ♦A, top of the solid sequence.

Suggested Play

South's goal is to take at least nine tricks. There are five sure tricks in spades, the ♥A, and ♣A. Two more tricks are required.

South browses Declarer's Checklist for ways to develop the extra tricks. Declarer has two more hearts than there are in dummy. This provides the opportunity to gain two tricks by trumping hearts in dummy.

```
DECLARER'S PLAN—THE ABC'S

Declarer: South      Contract: 3♠

ASSESS THE SITUATION
  Goal                    9
  Sure Tricks             7
  Extra Tricks Needed     2

BROWSE DECLARER'S CHECKLIST
  Promotion
  Length
  The Finesse
  Trumping in Dummy    2 in hearts

CONSIDER THE ORDER
  • Keep enough trumps in the
    dummy to trump two hearts.
```

In Considering the Order, declarer must be careful to keep at least two trumps in the dummy with which to ruff the hearts. Declarer may have to delay drawing all the trumps until the hearts are ruffed.

Suppose West takes two tricks with the ♦A and ♦K and then leads the ♦Q. South trumps the third round and can immediately play the ♥A and lead the ♥3 and trump it in dummy. Then declarer can take the ♠K and lead a spade to the ♠A. Now declarer leads the ♥9 and trumps in dummy. Since there are no spades left in dummy to draw the last trump, a low club is led to declarer's ♣A. Declarer can then draw West's remaining spade by playing the ♠J.

Conclusion

East-West can actually make 4♥ if they can reach that contract. As declarer in 4♥, East would lose only one spade trick, the ♥A, and ♣A. North's preemptive jump raise to 3♠ is effective in making it difficult for East-West to find their best contract.

If East and West do bid 4♥, South might choose to bid 4♠ with the knowledge that North has a weak hand but four-card trump support. Since 4♠ is only defeated one trick, it is a good sacrifice against East-West's game contract.

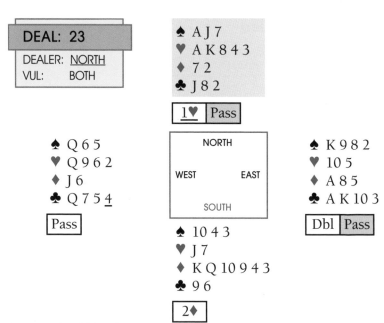

DEAL: 23

DEALER: NORTH
VUL: BOTH

♠ A J 7
♥ A K 8 4 3
♦ 7 2
♣ J 8 2

| 1♥ | Pass |

♠ Q 6 5
♥ Q 9 6 2
♦ J 6
♣ Q 7 5 4

NORTH

WEST   EAST

SOUTH

♠ K 9 8 2
♥ 10 5
♦ A 8 5
♣ A K 10 3

| Pass |

| Dbl | Pass |

♠ 10 4 3
♥ J 7
♦ K Q 10 9 4 3
♣ 9 6

| 2♦ |

Suggested Bidding

North deals and opens 1♥. North values the hand as 14 points: 13 high-card points plus 1 length point for the five-card heart suit. North opens the five-card major suit.

East doubles. With 14 high-card points plus 1 dummy point for the doubleton heart and support for the unbid suits, East's hand is suitable for a takeout double.

South bids 2♦. South has 6 high-card points plus 2 length points for the six-card diamond suit. If East had passed, South would not have enough strength to bid a new suit at the two level and would respond 1NT. After East's double, South can bid 2♦. A new suit at the two level is not forcing after the double. With 10 or more points, South would start with a redouble.

West passes. As advancer, West would have to bid if South passed. When South bids 2♦, West no longer has to bid. With only 7 high-card points, West doesn't have enough to compete to 3♣.

North passes. North has nothing extra for the opening bid and South's 2♦ is not forcing, so North can pass and settle for partscore.

East passes. With minimum values for the takeout double, East has nothing more to say and the auction is over. South is the declarer in 2♦.

Suggested Opening Lead

Against South's 2♦ contract, West doesn't have a clear cut choice of opening lead. West might choose the ♣4, fourth highest from a suit with no touching high cards.

Suggested Play

South's goal is to take eight tricks. There is one sure spade trick and there are two sure heart tricks. Five more tricks are needed.

Declarer browses the checklist.

Declarer can plan to develop five winners in the diamond suit through a combination of the finesse and length.

Suppose East wins the first two tricks with the ♣A-K and then leads another club. South can trump the third round of clubs and should now go after

DECLARER'S PLAN—THE ABC'S	
Declarer: South Contract: 2♦	
ASSESS THE SITUATION	
Goal	8
Sure Tricks	3
Extra Tricks Needed	5
BROWSE DECLARER'S CHECKLIST	
Promotion	
Length	4 in diamonds
The Finesse	1 in diamonds
Trumping in Dummy	
CONSIDER THE ORDER	
• Be in the right hand to lead toward the ♦K and ♦Q.	

diamonds. On the actual deal, declarer can lead the ♦K to drive out the ♦A and will then take five diamond tricks because the ♦J falls under the ♦Q.

A better approach is to lead toward the cards South hopes will take tricks, the ♦K and ♦Q, hoping East holds the ♦A. South plays the ♥7 to dummy's ♥K and leads a diamond toward the ♦K-Q. If East plays the ♦A, South can play low and later use the ♦K and ♦Q to draw the remaining trumps. If East plays low, South wins with the ♦Q (or ♦K). South then leads the ♥J to dummy's ♥A to lead another diamond. If East plays the ♦A, South plays low; if East plays low, South wins the ♦K. By playing diamonds in this fashion, declarer doesn't have to rely on the ♦J falling on the second round.

Conclusion

North and South do well to get to a partscore of 2♦ after East's takeout double. That's their best contract. If South were to bid 1NT instead of 2♦, for example, that contract can be defeated.

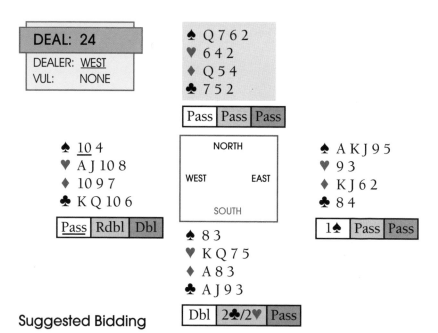

DEAL: 24

DEALER: WEST
VUL: NONE

♠ Q 7 6 2
♥ 6 4 2
♦ Q 5 4
♣ 7 5 2

| Pass | Pass | Pass |

♠ 10 4
♥ A J 10 8
♦ 10 9 7
♣ K Q 10 6

NORTH

WEST   EAST

SOUTH

♠ A K J 9 5
♥ 9 3
♦ K J 6 2
♣ 8 4

| Pass | Rdbl | Dbl |

| 1♠ | Pass | Pass |

♠ 8 3
♥ K Q 7 5
♦ A 8 3
♣ A J 9 3

Suggested Bidding

| Dbl | 2♣/2♥ | Pass |

West deals and passes. West has only 10 high-card points, not enough to open the bidding.

North passes. North has only 4 high-card points..

East opens 1♠. With 12 high-card points plus 1 length point for the five-card spade suit, East opens the bidding at the one level.

South doubles. South has support for the unbid suits and 14 high-card points plus 1 dummy point for the doubleton spade, enough for a takeout double.

West redoubles. West's redouble shows 10 or more high-card points and sends the message East and West have the majority of strength.

North passes. If West had passed, North would have to bid. After the redouble, North can pass with no real preference for any of the unbid suits.

East passes. West's redouble could be made with a variety of hands, so East passes, waiting to see how the auction will develop.

South bids one of the four-card suits, either 2♣ or 2♥. South doesn't want to defend 1♠ redoubled[41].

---

[41] The trick score for making 1♠ would be multiplied by four, making it enough for a game bonus. Also, overtricks would be worth 400 points each (see Appendix 2).

West doubles. Having redoubled, West can now make a penalty double of whichever suit South chooses. The penalty should be more than East-West would receive for making a partscore or game contract.

North, East, and South all pass with likely no better contract.

Suggested Opening Lead

Against South's doubled contract, West leads the ♠10, top of the doubleton in partner's suit.

Suggested Play

In a contract of 2♣ doubled (or 2♥ doubled), South's goal is to take eight tricks. South counts the sure tricks. There is one in diamonds and one in clubs. Six more tricks are needed.

South browses Declarer's Checklist. One winner can be promoted in the heart suit, but it's difficult to see where additional tricks will come from. South could try leading toward dummy's ♦Q, hoping West has the ♦K, but that doesn't work. South could hope

DECLARER'S PLAN—THE ABC'S	
Declarer: South	Contract: 2♣ Dbl
ASSESS THE SITUATION	
Goal	8
Sure Tricks	2
Extra Tricks Needed	6
BROWSE DECLARER'S CHECKLIST	
Promotion	1 in hearts
Length	1 in hearts
	or clubs?
The Finesse	1 in diamonds?
Trumping in Dummy	
CONSIDER THE ORDER	
• Take the tricks and run!	

the missing clubs or hearts are divided 3-3 and an extra trick can be developed through length but both suits divide 4-2.

On a deal like this, South will have difficulty taking more than three or four tricks without some help from the defense. West might lead the ♥A, for example, establishing two tricks for declarer. South will have to settle for whatever tricks are available.

Conclusion

This deal illustrates the potential danger in competing. There is nothing wrong with the takeout double but, when East-West hold the balance of strength, it's possible to run into a large penalty.

To get a large penalty, East and West have to make effective use of the redouble. That takes some cooperation and this deal shows how it can be done.

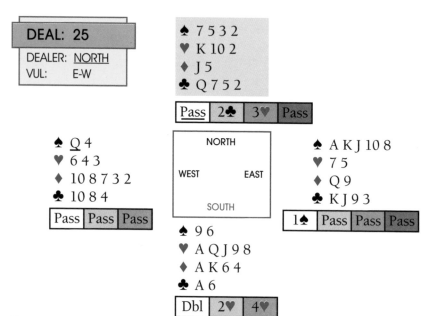

DEAL: 25

DEALER: NORTH
VUL: E-W

♠ 7 5 3 2
♥ K 10 2
♦ J 5
♣ Q 7 5 2

| Pass | 2♣ | 3♥ | Pass |

NORTH

WEST   EAST

SOUTH

♠ Q 4
♥ 6 4 3
♦ 10 8 7 3 2
♣ 10 8 4

| Pass | Pass | Pass |

♠ A K J 10 8
♥ 7 5
♦ Q 9
♣ K J 9 3

| 1♠ | Pass | Pass | Pass |

♠ 9 6
♥ A Q J 9 8
♦ A K 6 4
♣ A 6

| Dbl | 2♥ | 4♥ |

Suggested Bidding

North passes as dealer. North has only 6 high-card points.

East opens 1♠. East has 14 high-card points plus 1 length point for the five-card spade suit. With two doubletons, East opens the five-card major suit.

South doubles. South has 18 high-card points plus 1 length point for the five-card heart suit, for a total of 19 points. That's too much for a simple overcall of 2♥, which would be limited to about 12-17 points. Instead of overcalling, South starts with a takeout double.

West passes with only 2 high-card points and 1 length point for the five-card diamond suit.

North advances 2♣. North assumes South has a standard takeout double. With only 6 points, North bids 2♣, bidding the four-card suit at the cheapest level.

East passes. Having opened the bidding and getting no response from partner, East has nothing more to say.

South now shows the true nature of the hand by bidding 2♥. The double followed by the bid of a new suit shows a hand too strong to overcall, about 18 or more points.

West passes again.

North raises to 3♥. North has three-card support for hearts and knows South has a strong hand, so North can show some values.

East passes. South continues to 4♥, and the auction is over.

Suggested Opening Lead

Against South's 4♥ contract, West would lead the ♠Q, top of the doubleton in partner's bid suit.

Suggested Play

South's goal is to take ten tricks with hearts as the trump suit. There are five hearts, two diamonds, and one club trick. Two more tricks need to be developed.

South browses Declarer's Checklist. With more diamonds in declarer's hand than dummy, there is the opportunity to gain two tricks by trumping diamonds in dummy.

In Considering the Order, declarer wants to keep enough trumps in dummy to ruff the

DECLARER'S PLAN—THE ABC'S
Declarer: South   Contract: 4♥
ASSESS THE SITUATION
Goal   10
Sure Tricks   8
Extra Tricks Needed   2
BROWSE DECLARER'S CHECKLIST
Promotion
Length
The Finesse
Trumping in Dummy   2 in diamonds
CONSIDER THE ORDER
• Keep enough hearts in dummy to trump two diamonds.
• Trump high to avoid being over-trumped.

diamonds. That means declarer has to delay drawing trumps.

Suppose the defenders win the first two spade tricks and East leads a third round. South trumps with the ♥8. Declarer can afford to take one round of trumps by playing the ♥A, but that's all for now. Declarer next takes the ♦A-K and leads a third round and trumps with dummy's ♥10. Even though East has no more diamonds, East has no heart higher than the ♥10 with which to overruff. Declarer can now play a low club from dummy to the ♣A and lead a fourth round of diamonds to trump with dummy's ♥K. Declarer still has two high hearts left to make ten tricks.

Conclusion

If South were to overcall 2♥, North-South might miss a game contract if North doesn't raise. To show a hand too strong for a simple overcall, South doubles first and then bids the suit.

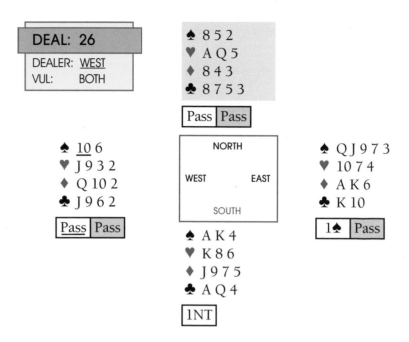

Suggested Bidding

West deals and passes with only 4 high-card points.

North passes with only 6 high-card points in second position.

East opens the bidding 1♠. East has 13 high-card points plus 1 length point for the five-card spade suit, enough to open at the one level.

South overcalls 1NT. South has a balanced hand with 17 high-card points. If East had passed, South would open 1NT. After East's 1♠ opening, South, with some strength in spades, can still show the same type of hand by overcalling 1NT.

West passes. West doesn't have enough for a response to East's 1♠ opening bid.

North passes. North doesn't have enough to take the partnership any higher after South's 1NT overcall.

East passes, having already shown the hand with the opening bid. That ends the auction and South is the declarer in a 1NT contract.

Suggested Opening Lead

Against South's 1NT contract, West would lead the ♠10, top of the doubleton in partner's suit.

Suggested Play

North puts down dummy and South makes a plan. South's goal is to take at least seven tricks. There are two sure tricks in spades, three in hearts, and one in clubs. One more trick is required.

South browses Declarer's Checklist. The club suit provides the possibility of an extra trick through a finesse. South can hope East holds the ♣K and can then take two tricks with the ♣A-Q rather than one.

> ### DECLARER'S PLAN—THE ABC'S
>
> Declarer: South   Contract: 1NT
>
> **A**SSESS THE SITUATION
> Goal   7
> Sure Tricks   6
> Extra Tricks Needed   1
>
> **B**ROWSE DECLARER'S CHECKLIST
> Promotion
> Length
> The Finesse   1 in clubs
> Trumping in Dummy
>
> **C**ONSIDER THE ORDER
> • Be in the right place at the right time to lead toward the ♣Q.

To take a finesse in clubs, declarer must be in the right place at the right time to lead toward the ♣Q. After winning a trick with the ♠K, declarer can play a low heart to North's ♥Q or ♥A. Now declarer is in the right hand to try the club finesse.

Declarer leads a low club from dummy and, when East plays the ♣10, declarer finesses the ♣Q. Since West doesn't hold the ♣K, the ♣Q wins and declarer has the extra trick needed to make the contract. It wouldn't help East to play the ♣K when a low club is led from dummy, South would win the ♣A and have the ♣Q as a second trick in the suit. After the club finesse works, declarer can take the remaining winners to make the contract.

Conclusion

A 1NT overcall is similar to a 1NT opening bid. Advancer bids in the same way as when responding to a 1NT opening. Advancer decides How High and Where the partnership belongs.

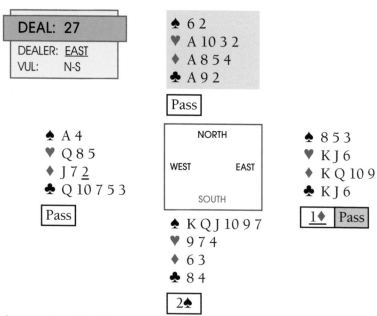

DEAL: 27

DEALER: EAST
VUL: N-S

North:
♠ 6 2
♥ A 10 3 2
♦ A 8 5 4
♣ A 9 2

Pass

West:
♠ A 4
♥ Q 8 5
♦ J 7 2
♣ Q 10 7 5 3

Pass

East:
♠ 8 5 3
♥ K J 6
♦ K Q 10 9
♣ K J 6

1♦ | Pass

South:
♠ K Q J 10 9 7
♥ 9 7 4
♦ 6 3
♣ 8 4

2♠

Suggested Bidding

East deals and opens 1♦. East has 13 high-card points. With no five-card major suit, East opens 1♦, the longer minor suit.

South makes a preemptive jump overcall of 2♠. South has only 6 high-card points but a good six-card suit. With five playing tricks, South can make a weak jump overcall to both describe the hand and take away bidding room from East-West.

West passes. West has 9 high-card points plus 1 length point for the five-card club suit, but that's not enough strength to bid a new suit at the three level. The hand is also unsuitable for a negative double because West doesn't have four-card support for the unbid major, hearts. West might bid 2NT, but this tends to show 11-12 points.

North passes. North has 12 high-card points, but not enough to bid anything after South's weak jump overcall. North can provide three tricks, but that won't be enough for the partnership to make 4♠ since South is showing only about five playing tricks. The partnership is high enough.

East passes. East has nothing more to say with a minimum opening bid and a balanced hand.

East's pass ends the auction and South is the declarer in 2♠.

Suggested Opening Lead

Against South's 2♠ contract, West would lead the ♦2, low from three cards in partner's bid suit.

Suggested Play

After West's ♦2 lead, North puts down dummy and South's goal is to take eight tricks with spades as trumps. There is one sure trick in hearts, one in diamonds, and one in clubs. Five more tricks are needed.

Declarer browses the checklist. Declarer can plan to develop five winners in the spade suit through promotion.

After winning the first trick, declarer can immediately lead a spade, planning to drive out the defenders' ♠A. This serves two purposes: promoting winners in the spade suit and drawing trumps.

DECLARER'S PLAN—THE ABC'S	
Declarer: South	Contract: 2♠
ASSESS THE SITUATION	
Goal	8
Sure Tricks	3
Extra Tricks Needed	5
BROWSE DECLARER'S CHECKLIST	
Promotion	5 in spades
Length	
The Finesse	
Trumping in Dummy	
CONSIDER THE ORDER	
• Draw trumps first.	
• Develop the extra spade tricks early.	

After West wins the ♠A, the defenders can take a diamond trick, but whatever they lead next can be won by declarer. Declarer draws the remaining trumps and takes five spade tricks to go with the ♥A, ♦A, and ♣A to make the contract.

Conclusion

South's jump overcall is a little risky since North-South are vulnerable and East-West are not. With such a solid spade suit, however, it's unlikely East-West will make a penalty double. The value of the preemptive jump overcall is it may keep East-West out of the auction. East-West can make 2NT or 3♣ but it isn't easy to get there after South's interference.

North should not consider playing in notrump. If the defenders hold up taking the ♠A for one round, North will get only one trick from the spade suit to go with the three aces.

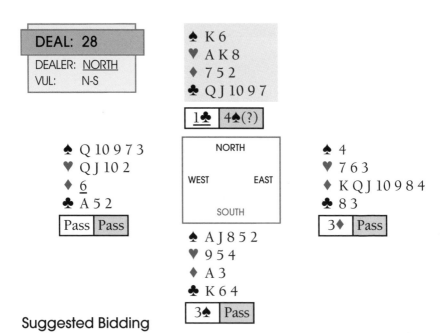

DEAL: 28
DEALER: NORTH
VUL: N-S

♠ K 6
♥ A K 8
♦ 7 5 2
♣ Q J 10 9 7

| 1♣ | 4♠(?) |

NORTH

WEST   EAST

SOUTH

♠ Q 10 9 7 3
♥ Q J 10 2
♦ 6
♣ A 5 2

| Pass | Pass |

♠ 4
♥ 7 6 3
♦ K Q J 10 9 8 4
♣ 8 3

| 3♦ | Pass |

♠ A J 8 5 2
♥ 9 5 4
♦ A 3
♣ K 6 4

| 3♠ | Pass |

Suggested Bidding

North deals and opens 1♣. North has 14 valuation points: 13 high-card points plus 1 length point for the five-card club suit. With no five-card major, North opens the five-card minor.

East overcalls 3♦. East has only 6 high-card points but an excellent seven-card suit. East can make a weak jump overcall, hoping to make the auction challenging for the opponents.

South bids 3♠. South has 12 high-card points plus 1 length point for the five-card spade suit. South would have responded 1♠ if East had passed. The 3♦ overcall makes South's call more challenging. South will probably choose to bid 3♠, forcing, showing a five-card or longer spade suit.

West passes. West has 9 high-card points plus 1 length point for the five-card spade suit, and no fit for partner's diamond suit.

North raises to 4♠. North is awkwardly placed over South's forcing 3♠ bid. North doesn't have strength in diamonds, so 3NT is unattractive. It isn't particularly attractive to rebid the five-card club suit at the four level. North might choose to raise partner's spades to game, even with only two spades. South has at least a five-card suit and perhaps six or more.

Everyone passes, and South is the declarer in 4♠.

Suggested Opening Lead

Against South's 4♠ contract, West would lead the ♦6, the singleton in partner's suit.

Suggested Play

South's goal is to take ten tricks with spades as trumps. There are two spade tricks, two hearts, and one diamond. Five more tricks are needed.

South browses Declarer's Checklist. South can plan to promote extra tricks in clubs. However, the key will be to avoid losing three tricks in the trump suit. South can hope East holds the ♠Q and may get an extra trick by finessing the ♠J. South may also get extra spade tricks through length, if the missing spades divide 3-3 or 4-2.

```
DECLARER'S PLAN—THE ABC'S

Declarer: South      Contract: 4♠

ASSESS THE SITUATION
  Goal                 10
  Sure Tricks           5
  Extra Tricks Needed   5

BROWSE DECLARER'S CHECKLIST
  Promotion         4 in clubs
  Length            2 in spades?
  The Finesse       1 in spades
  Trumping in Dummy

CONSIDER THE ORDER
  • Draw trumps.
  • Play the high card from the short
    side first when promoting clubs.
```

East's 3♦ bid, showing a long diamond suit and a weak hand makes it unlikely East holds the ♠Q or the six missing spades will divide favorably. On the actual layout, West has three spade winners to go with the ♣A, enough to defeat the contract. Declarer will be able to promote winners in dummy's club suit and use them to discard a heart and a diamond, but that's the best South can do.

Conclusion

This deal illustrates the effectiveness of the weak jump overcall. A jump to 3♦ by East is more effective than a jump to 2♦ and could push North-South into a poor contract. North-South can make 3NT, but it is difficult to get there after East's interference.

If North-South were to double 3♦, they would defeat the contract only one trick. East can promote six diamond tricks and a heart trick to go along with the ♣A.

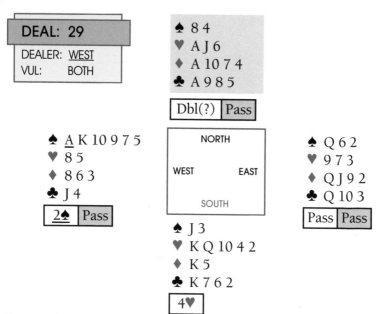

DEAL: 29

DEALER: WEST
VUL: BOTH

♠ 8 4
♥ A J 6
♦ A 10 7 4
♣ A 9 8 5

Dbl(?) Pass

♠ A K 10 9 7 5
♥ 8 5
♦ 8 6 3
♣ J 4

2♠ Pass

NORTH

WEST   EAST

SOUTH

♠ Q 6 2
♥ 9 7 3
♦ Q J 9 2
♣ Q 10 3

Pass Pass

♠ J 3
♥ K Q 10 4 2
♦ K 5
♣ K 7 6 2

4♥

Suggested Bidding

West deals and opens 2♠. West has 8 high-card points plus 2 length points for the six-card spade suit. With a good six-card suit and less than the values for an opening bid at the one level, West opens with a weak two-bid.

North doubles. North has 13 high-card points and support for the unbid suits. North can add 1 dummy point for the doubleton spade. Although the auction is already at the two level and North has only three-card support for hearts, North will probably choose to make a takeout double. West's preemptive opening has created a challenge for North and South and, if they don't take some risk, they may be effectively shut out of the auction.

East has a weak hand but does have three-card support for spades, so East might choose to further West's preemptive action by raising to the level corresponding to the combined number of trumps. With a balanced hand and only queens and jacks, however, some East players might prefer to pass, especially when vulnerable.

South advances 4♥. South, as advancer, has 12 high-card points plus 1 length point for the five-card heart suit. North has promised at least an opening bid with the takeout double – perhaps a little more since the double was at the two level.

That's enough for South to know HOW HIGH. The partnership has enough combined strength for game. South also knows WHERE. South can bid 4♥ with the knowledge North's double has shown support for hearts.

Everyone passes, and South is the declarer in 4♥.

Suggested Opening Lead

West leads the ♠A, top of the touching high cards, against 4♥.

Suggested Play

South's goal is to take ten tricks with hearts as the trump suit.

There are five heart tricks, two diamond tricks, and two club tricks. One more trick needs to be developed.

South browses Declarer's Checklist. There are eight clubs between the combined hands, so the club suit might provide an extra trick through length if the five missing clubs are divided 3-2.

DECLARER'S PLAN—THE ABC'S	
Declarer: South	Contract: 4♥
ASSESS THE SITUATION	
Goal	10
Sure Tricks	9
Extra Tricks Needed	1
BROWSE DECLARER'S CHECKLIST	
Promotion	
Length	1 in clubs
The Finesse	
Trumping in Dummy	
CONSIDER THE ORDER	
• Draw trumps first.	
• Take the loss early in clubs.	

The defenders may take the first two spade tricks and lead a diamond. Declarer wins, and the first priority is to draw the defenders' trumps. Declarer then goes about establishing the extra trick in clubs while still holding winners in the other suits to regain the lead.

Declarer takes the ♣A and ♣K. When both defenders follow suit, there is only one club outstanding. Declarer leads another club, giving up a trick to East's ♣Q. Declarer now has the rest of the tricks since declarer's remaining club is a winner.

Conclusion

West's weak 2♠ opening presents a challenge to North-South. If they don't enter the auction, West will buy the contract in 2♠ and take at least six tricks, perhaps seven if the defenders don't trump one of the potential diamond winners. Down two, even doubled, would be a good result for East-West since North-South can make a game contract.

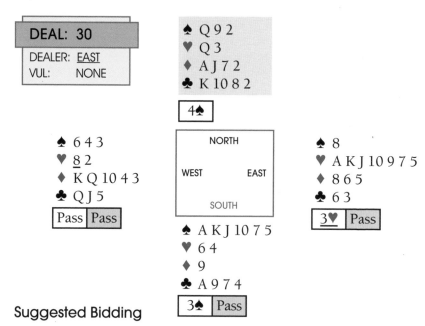

DEAL: 30

DEALER: EAST
VUL: NONE

♠ Q 9 2
♥ Q 3
♦ A J 7 2
♣ K 10 8 2

4♠

NORTH

WEST   EAST

SOUTH

♠ 6 4 3
♥ 8 2
♦ K Q 10 4 3
♣ Q J 5

Pass | Pass

♠ 8
♥ A K J 10 9 7 5
♦ 8 6 5
♣ 6 3

3♥ | Pass

♠ A K J 10 7 5
♥ 6 4
♦ 9
♣ A 9 7 4

3♠ | Pass

Suggested Bidding

East is the dealer and opens the bidding 3♥. With only 8 high-card points plus 3 length points for the seven-card heart suit, East doesn't have enough to open the bidding at the one level. With a good seven-card suit, however, East can make a preemptive opening bid at the three level. This is both a descriptive bid and also takes away a lot of bidding room from the opponents, making it more difficult for them to reach their best contract if the deal belongs to them.

South overcalls 3♠. South has 12 high-card points plus 2 length points for the six-card spade suit. If East had passed, South would have opened 1♠. After East's preemptive opening bid, South has to choose between passing and overcalling. With a good six-card suit and opening-bid values, South can overcall even though it is at the three level.

West passes. West has only 8 high-card points plus 1 length point for the five-card diamond suit. East has shown a weak hand, and West doesn't have enough support to further the preempt by raising.

North advances to 4♠. North has three-card support for spades and 12 high-card points plus 1 dummy point for the doubleton heart. Since South should have at least opening-bid values to overcall at the three level, there should be enough combined strength for game.

Everyone passes, and the auction is over with South as the declarer in 4♠.

Suggested Opening Lead

Against South's 4♠ contract, West will lead the ♥8, top of the doubleton in partner's suit.

Suggested Play

South's goal is to take ten or more tricks to make 4♠. South begins by counting the sure winners: six spades, one diamond, and two clubs, for a total of nine tricks. One more trick is needed.

South browses Declarer's Checklist. The club suit might provide an extra trick through length after giving up a club trick if the five missing clubs in the defenders' hands are divided 3-2.

```
DECLARER'S PLAN—THE ABC'S

Declarer: South      Contract: 4♠

ASSESS THE SITUATION
   Goal                    10
   Sure Tricks              9
   Extra Tricks Needed      1

BROWSE DECLARER'S CHECKLIST
   Promotion
   Length              1 in clubs
   The Finesse
   Trumping in Dummy

CONSIDER THE ORDER
   • Draw trumps.
   • Take the loss early in clubs.
```

East will likely win the first two heart tricks. If East then leads a diamond, West will play the ♦Q and declarer can win dummy's ♦A.

Declarer draws the defenders' trumps. This takes three rounds since the defenders' four trumps divide 3-1. After that, declarer can tackle the club suit. Declarer plays the ♣A and ♣K. When both defenders follow suit each time, there is only one club outstanding. Declarer gives up a trick to the defenders' high club, West's ♣Q. That establishes declarer's remaining club as a winning trick. Declarer still has plenty of trumps to regain the lead and take the established club winner, making the contract.

Conclusion

Preemptive opening bids can be effective since they take bidding room away from the opponents. It is possible to compete with an overcall after the preemptive opening but, the higher the level, the more strength is needed. For an overcall at the two level or higher, at least opening-bid values are needed, along with a good suit, preferably a six-card or longer suit.

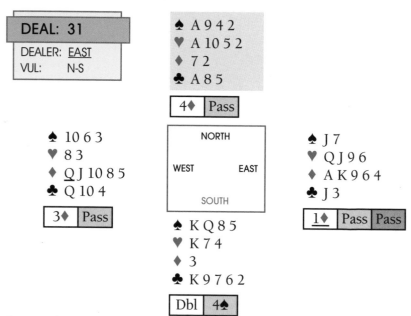

Suggested Bidding

East is the dealer and opens 1♦. East has 12 high-card points plus 1 length point for the five-card diamond suit. With no five-card major suit, East opens the longer minor suit.

South doubles. South has a close decision on how to enter the auction. South has 11 high-card points and could add 1 length point for the five-card club suit. South might overcall 2♣, but the suit isn't very good. With support for the unbid suits, a better choice is to add 3 dummy points for the singleton diamond and make a takeout double.

West raises to 3♦. With five-card support for East's suit, West can value the hand as 5 high-card points plus 1 dummy point for the doubleton heart. With 6 points, West could simply raise to 2♦ after South's double but, with such a weak hand, might choose to make a preemptive jump raise to 3♦.

North bids 4♦. North, as advancer, has 12 high-card points and, since South is showing an opening bid or more with the takeout double, knows How High, game. North isn't quite sure about Where. The partnership could belong in 4♥ or 4♠. To get more information, North can cuebid the opponents' suit, 4♦. This is advancer's forcing bid.

East passes, and South bids 4♠. South chooses 4♠ since South has four spades and only three hearts. South's 4♠ call will likely end the auction with South as the declarer in 4♠.

Suggested Opening Lead

Against South's 4♠, West would lead the ♦Q, top of the touching honors in the partnership's suit.

Suggested Play

South's goal as declarer is to take ten tricks. There are three sure spade tricks, two hearts, and two clubs. Three more tricks are needed.

Declarer browses the checklist. If the five missing spades are divided 3-2, the spade suit will provide an extra trick through length. Similarly, if the five missing clubs are divided 3-2, the club suit will provide two extra tricks through length.

In Considering the Order, declarer wants to start by drawing the defenders' trumps and then establish the extra club winners early.

DECLARER'S PLAN—THE ABC'S		
Declarer: South	Contract: 4♠	
ASSESS THE SITUATION		
Goal	10	
Sure Tricks	7	
Extra Tricks Needed	3	
BROWSE DECLARER'S CHECKLIST		
Promotion		
Length	1 in spades	
	2 in clubs	
The Finesse		
Trumping in Dummy		
CONSIDER THE ORDER		
• Draw trumps first.		
• Take the loss early in clubs.		

Suppose the defenders win the first diamond trick and play a second round of diamonds. South can trump and play the ♠K, ♠Q, and a low spade to the ♠A to draw the defenders' trumps. Then declarer can take the ♣A, ♣K, and lead a third round of clubs to establish South's two remaining clubs as winners. West wins the ♣Q, but whatever suit West leads next, declarer can win and get to the South hand with the ♥K to take the two club winners.

Conclusion

North could guess whether to bid 4♥ or 4♠ opposite South's takeout double but that could lead to the wrong contract. The cuebid is an effective tool to get the partnership to the best contract when advancer needs more information to decide HOW HIGH and WHERE.

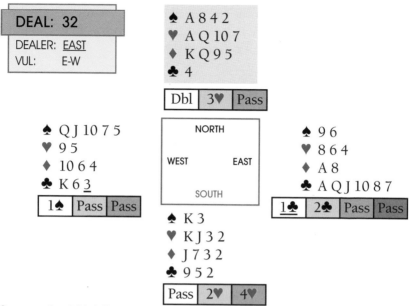

DEAL: 32

DEALER: EAST
VUL: E-W

♠ A 8 4 2
♥ A Q 10 7
♦ K Q 9 5
♣ 4

| Dbl | 3♥ | Pass |

♠ Q J 10 7 5
♥ 9 5
♦ 10 6 4
♣ K 6 3

| 1♠ | Pass | Pass |

NORTH

WEST   EAST

SOUTH

♠ 9 6
♥ 8 6 4
♦ A 8
♣ A Q J 10 8 7

| 1♣ | 2♣ | Pass | Pass |

♠ K 3
♥ K J 3 2
♦ J 7 3 2
♣ 9 5 2

| Pass | 2♥ | 4♥ |

Suggested Bidding

East deals and opens 1♣. East has 11 high-card points plus 2 length points for the six-card club suit, for a total of 13, enough to open at the one level in the six-card minor suit.

South passes. South has only 8 high-card points and no five-card or longer suit to overcall.

West responds 1♠. West has 6 high-card points plus 1 length point for the five-card spade suit. West responds 1♠, showing 6 or more points and four or more spades.

North doubles. North has support for both unbid suits, hearts and diamonds. With 15 high-card points and 3 dummy points for the singleton club, North can make a takeout double.

East rebids 2♣. East doesn't have support for spades and doesn't have a balanced hand. East rebids the clubs to show the extra length in the suit.

South advances 2♥. South doesn't have to bid after East bids 2♣ but, with 8 points, wants to compete once North invites South into the auction. With four hearts and four diamonds, South bids 2♥, the major suit.

West passes. West doesn't have anything extra for the initial response, but West might compete to 3♣.

North raises to 3♥. North has 18 points, enough to consider going for the game bonus.

East passes, and South bids 4♥, accepting partner's invitation to go for the game bonus.

Everyone passes, and South is the declarer in 4♥.

Suggested Opening Lead

Against South's 4♥ contract, West leads the ♣3, low from three or more cards in the suit bid by partner.

Suggested Play

South's goal is to take ten tricks. There are two spade tricks and four heart tricks. Four more tricks are needed.

The diamonds provide an opportunity to promote two winners and develop a third trick through length. Since declarer has more clubs than dummy, declarer can also plan to trump two clubs in dummy to gain two tricks.

In Considering the Order, declarer wants to keep enough hearts in dummy to trump the clubs. Declarer also wants to

DECLARER'S PLAN—THE ABC'S	
Declarer: South	Contract: 4♥
ASSESS THE SITUATION	
Goal	10
Sure Tricks	6
Extra Tricks Needed	4
BROWSE DECLARER'S CHECKLIST	
Promotion	2 in diamonds
Length	1 in diamonds
The Finesse	
Trumping in Dummy	2 in clubs
CONSIDER THE ORDER	
• Leave enough trumps in dummy to trump two clubs.	
• Draw trumps.	
• Take the loss early when promoting tricks in diamonds.	

promote the diamond winners but needs to draw the trumps before taking the established winners.

This is a lot to do, so declarer may not be able to do everything but should still finish with ten tricks. If East wins the first trick with the ♣A and leads a spade, for example, declarer can win and draw three rounds of trumps. Then declarer can promote the diamond winners by giving up a trick to the ♦A. Declarer will have only one trump left in dummy and can trump only one club, but will still have ten tricks.

Conclusion

Even after East opens the bidding and West responds, North-South can reach their game contract with the help of a takeout double.

Appendices

Appendix 1 – Declarer's Plan

When the auction is over, the opening lead is made, and dummy is placed face up on the table, declarer should make a plan for taking enough tricks to make the contract. There are three suggested stages, the ABC's:

> ### Declarer's Plan – The ABC's
>
> A – Assess the Situation
> B – Browse Declarer's Checklist to Develop Extra tricks
> C – Consider the Order

Assess the Situation

This stage can be divided into three steps:

1) Goal. Start by considering the number of tricks required to make the contract. In 4♥, for example, declarer needs to take ten tricks.

2) Sure Tricks[42]. Count the sure tricks, or winners – those that can be taken without giving up the lead. An ace is a sure trick; an ace and king in the same suit are two sure tricks.

3) Extra Tricks Needed. Compare the number of tricks needed to the sure tricks. If there are eight sure tricks in a contract of 4♥, for example, two more are needed.

---

[42] In a trump contract, declarer can also count losers – the tricks that could be lost to the defenders.

Browse Declarer's Checklist to Develop Extra Tricks

When there aren't enough sure tricks to make the contract, declarer looks at the various techniques for developing, or establishing, extra tricks:

Declarer's Checklist	
Promotion	
Length	
The Finesse	
Trumping in Dummy	

The first three methods are available in both notrump and trump contracts. The fourth is available only in trump contracts.

Promotion

Declarer can sometimes turn cards into winners by driving out the higher-ranking cards. For example:

DUMMY ♥ 4 2

DECLARER ♥ K Q

Declarer can lead the ♥K, or ♥Q, to drive out the defenders' ♥A and promote the remaining high card into a winner.

Length

Declarer can sometimes turn low cards into winners by driving out all the defenders' cards in the suit. For example:

DUMMY ♦ 9 6 3

DECLARER ♦ A K 7 5 2

Declarer can take two sure tricks with the ♦A and ♦K and then lead a third round of diamonds, giving up a trick to the defenders. If the five missing diamonds are divided 3-2, declarer's two remaining diamonds are winners.

In predicting how many tricks can be developed from a suit through length, declarer can use the guideline:

So, when five cards are missing, declarer can expect them to divide evenly, 3-2. If six cards are missing, declarer can expect them to divide slightly unevenly, 4-2. There is no guarantee when developing tricks through length. Five missing cards could be divided 4-1 or 5-0. Six missing cards could be divided 3-3, 5-1, or 6-0.

The Finesse

Declarer can sometimes develop tricks with high cards when the defenders hold higher-ranking cards.

DUMMY
♠ A Q

DECLARER
♠ 7 6

The ♠A is a sure trick, but the ♠Q is not since the defenders have the ♠K. However, declarer can hope to take two tricks by leading a low spade toward dummy and playing – finessing – dummy's ♠Q. If the ♠K is favorably placed on declarer's left, the ♠Q will win. If the ♠K is unfavorably placed on declarer's right, the finesse will lose and declarer will get only one trick.

A general guideline for taking finesses is to lead toward the card you hope will take a trick.

Trumping in Dummy

In a trump contract, declarer can sometimes gain a trick by using dummy's trump.

DUMMY
♥ 7 5 3
♣ 6

DECLARER
♥ A K Q J 10
♣ A 7

The trump suit is hearts. If declarer takes the five heart winners and the ♣A, declarer gets six tricks. If declarer plays the ♣A and then leads the ♣7 and trumps it in dummy, declarer gets seven tricks: the ♣A, the ruff, and the five heart winners. Declarer gains a trick by trumping in dummy.

Consider the Order

When developing and taking tricks, the order in which the tricks are played can be important. Here are some considerations:

1) Take the tricks and run. With enough sure tricks to make the contract, declarer should generally take them.

2) Draw trumps. In a trump contract, declarer should draw the defenders' trumps by playing the trump suit until the defenders have none left, unless declarer needs the trump suit for other purposes, such as trumping in dummy.

3) Keep enough trumps in dummy. When planning on trumping in dummy, declarer may have to delay drawing trumps to keep enough trumps in dummy.

4) Develop extra tricks early. To develop extra tricks, one or more tricks may have to be lost. Declarer should not be afraid to lose such tricks early, while keeping sure tricks in the other suits to regain the lead and then take the established winners.

5) Be in the right place at the right time. Declarer must often plan to be in the appropriate hand to take or establish winners.

6) Play the high card from the short side first. When taking sure tricks or promoting winners in suits that are unevenly divided between the hands, it's usually a good idea to start by playing the high cards from the hand with the fewer cards.

Appendix 2 – Scoring

A partnership scores points in three ways:

- Trick score.
- Bonuses.
- Penalties.

The trick score and penalty points are the same for all formats of the game, but the bonus points can vary. There are also variations in the score depending on the vulnerability and whether the contract is *undoubled*, doubled, or redoubled.

Trick Score

A partnership that makes a contract scores points for the tricks bid and made as follows:

	Clubs (♣) or Diamonds (♦)	Hearts (♥) or Spades (♠)	Notrump
First Trick	20	30	40
Subsequent Tricks	20	30	30

- The trick score only applies to tricks taken beyond the initial six tricks assumed in the contract.
- If the contract is doubled and made, the trick score is doubled.
- If the contract is redoubled and made, the trick score is quadrupled.

Game is a total trick score of 100 or more points. A game can be scored in a single deal by bidding and making the following contracts.

<table>
<tr><td colspan="3" align="center">Game Contracts</td></tr>
<tr><td>Game in Notrump</td><td>3NT (nine tricks)</td><td>40 + 30 + 30 = 100</td></tr>
<tr><td>Game in a Major</td><td>4♥ or 4♠ (ten tricks)</td><td>30 + 30 + 30 + 30 = 120</td></tr>
<tr><td>Game in a Minor</td><td>5♦ or 5♣ (eleven tricks)</td><td>20 + 20 + 20 + 20 + 20 = 100</td></tr>
</table>

A contract that is worth less than 100 points is called a partscore.

Bonus Points

GAME AND PARTGAME BONUS (DUPLICATE BRIDGE)

In duplicate bridge, each deal is scored separately. There is no carryover from one deal to the next. The bonuses for bidding and making contracts are awarded as follows:

- 300 for bidding and making a game contract when non-vulnerable.

- 500 for bidding and making a game contract when vulnerable.

- 50 for bidding and making a partscore contract.

SLAM BONUS (ALL FORMATS)

	Non-Vulnerable	Vulnerable
Small Slam (12 tricks)	500	750
Grand Slam (13 tricks)	1000	1500

OVERTRICKS (ALL FORMATS)

For each extra trick delcarer makes in a contract:

Notrump	30 points per trick
Major Suit	30 points per trick
Minor Suit	20 points per trick

MAKING A DOUBLED OR REDOUBLED CONTRACT (ALL FORMATS)

For making a doubled contract, there is a bonus of 50 points. For making a redoubled contract, there is a bonus of 100 points:

Penalty Points

For each trick by which declarer falls short of the contract (undertrick):

	Non-Vulnerable			Vulnerable		
	Undoubled	Doubled	Redoubled	Undoubled	Doubled	Redoubled
First Trick	50	100	200	100	200	400
Second Trick	50	200	400	100	300	600
Third Trick	50	200	400	100	300	600
Each Subsequent Trick	50	300	600	100	300	600

Glossary

Advancer – The partner of a player who makes an overcall or takeout double. (page 45)

Auction – The process of determining the contract through a series of bids. (page 2)

Balanced Hand – A hand with no voids, no singletons, and no more than one doubleton. (page 52)

Bidding Ladder – The order in which bids can be made, starting with 1♣ and ending with 7NT. (pages 2, 4)

Bonus – Points scored for making a partscore, game, or slam or for defeating the opponents' contract. (pages 8, 19)

Call – Any bid, double, redouble or pass. (page 8)

Chicago – A form of the game which is played in units of four deals. (page 147)

Competitive Auction – An auction in which both sides are bidding to try and win the contract. (page 37)

Competitive Bidding – Entering the auction after the other side has opened the bidding. (page 3)

Combined Hands – Both hands belonging to one partnership. (page 23)

Contract – The undertaking by declarer's side to win at least a specific number of tricks in a specific denomination as determined by the final bid in the auction. (page 1)

Conventional – A bid which conveys a meaning other than what would normally be attributed to it. (page 17)

Cuebid (in the Opponent's Suit) – An artificial forcing bid in a suit bid by the opponents. It can be used by responder after an opponent overcalls and by advancer after partner overcalls or makes a takeout double. (pages 47, 48)

Deal – The distribution of the cards to the four players. (page 19)

Declarer – The player from the side that won the auction who first bid the denomination named in the contract. (page 3)

Defeat – Stop declarer from making a contract. (page 2)

Defense – The side that did not win the auction. (page 38)

Denomination – The suit, or notrump, specified in a bid. (page 19)

Discard – Play a card to a trick which is from a different suit than the one led and is not a trump. (page 81)

Distribution – The number of cards held in each suit by a particular player; the number of cards held in a particular suit by the partnership. (pages 39, 54)

Double – A call that increases the bonus for making or defeating a contract. It can also be used to ask partner to bid a suit. (page 21)

Doubleton – A holding of two cards in a suit. (pages 14, 45)

Draw Trump – Playing the trump suit until the opponents have none left. (pages 29, 75)

Dummy Points – Points used in place of length points when valuing a hand in support of partner's suit: void, 5 points; singleton, 3 points; doubleton, 1 point. (page 45)

Duplicate – A form of the game in which the same deal is played more than once. (page 20)

Establish – Set up sure tricks by driving out winning cards in the opponents' hands. (page 13)

Feature – A potentially useful high card, such as an ace or a king, in a suit. A feature can be shown after opening a weak two-bid when responder uses the artificial 2NT response. (page 17)

Finesse – A method of building extra tricks by trapping an opponent's high card(s). (pages 29, 33)

Fit – Ideally, three-card or longer support for a suit bid by partner. A combined partnership holding of eight or more cards in a suit will usually be a suitable trump fit. (page 10)

Forcing (Bid) – A bid partner is not expected to pass. (page 14)

Fourth Highest – A lead of the fourth card down from the top in a suit. (page 35)

Game – A total trick score of 100 or more points. (pages 4, 7)

Game Contract – A contract which has a trick score value of 100 or more points. (page 10)

Game Bonus – The bonus awarded for bidding and making a game contract. (page 8)

Go Down – Be defeated in a contract. For example, 'down three' would indicate that the contract was defeated by three tricks. (page 147)

Grand Slam – A contract to take all thirteen tricks. (page 20)

Hand Valuation – The method to determine the value of a particular hand during the auction. Usually a combination of high card strength and suit length or shortness. (page 39)

HCPs – An abbreviation for high-card points. (page 1)

High Card – One of the top four cards in a suit: ace, king, queen, or jack. (page 1)

High Card Points – The value of high cards in a hand: ace, 4; king, 3; queen, 2; jack, 1. (page 1)

Honor (Card) – An ace, king, queen, jack, or ten. (page 2)

How High – The level at which the contract should be played. (page 3)

Invitational – A bid which encourages partner to continue bidding. (page 56)

Jump Overcall – An overcall at a level higher than necessary. For example, 2♠ would be a jump overcall over an opening bid of 1♥ because it is only necessary to bid 1♠. A jump overcall is typically used as a preemptive bid. (page 64)

Law of Total Tricks – An observation that the total number of tricks that can be taken by both sides is usually equal to the combined length of each side's best trump suit. It results in a guideline for competitive auctions: The partnership should generally compete to a level corresponding to the number of combined trumps held by the partnership (e.g. with 9 combined trumps, compete to the 3 level - 9 tricks). (pages 7, 9)

Length Points – The valuation assigned to long suits in a hand: five-card suit, 1 point; six-card suit, 2 points; seven-card suit, 3 points; eight-card suit, 4 points. (page 3)

Link Card – A card which can be led to a winner – entry – in the opposite hand. (page 12)

Major (Suit) – Spades or hearts. (page 14)

Minor (Suit) – Diamonds or clubs. (page 16)

Negative Double (Responder's Double) – A takeout double by responder after partner opens one of a suit and the next player overcalls in a suit. (pages 124, 132)

New Suit – A suit which has not previously been bid in the auction. (page 11)

Non-Vulnerable – In rubber bridge, a partnership that has not won a game. In duplicate or Chicago scoring, the vulnerability is assigned to each deal. The bonuses and penalties are less when a partnership is non-vulnerable than when it is vulnerable. (page 20)

One Level – The lowest level at which the auction can start. It represents seven tricks. (page 1)

Opening Lead – The card led to the first trick. The player to declarer's left leads first. (page 2)

Overcall – A bid made after the opponents have opened the bidding. (page 37)

Overtrick – A trick won by declarer in excess of the number required to make the contract. (page 20)

Partscore – A contract that does not receive a game bonus if made. (page 18)

Pattern – The number of cards held in each suit in a player's hand. (page 86)

Penalty – The bonus awarded to the defenders for defeating a contract. (page 19, 21)

Penalty Double – A double made with the expectation of defeating the opponents' contract. Partner is expected to pass. (pages 79, 132)

Preemptive Jump Raise – A raise of partner's suit one or more levels higher than necessary to show a weak hand with good trump support. Typically used by responder after right-hand opponent overcalls or makes a takeout double, or by advancer after partner overcalls in a suit. (page 46)

Preemptive Opening Bid – An opening bid in a suit of 2♦ or higher. Preemptive opening bids describe a weak hand with a good long suit and are designed to make it more challenging for the opponents to enter the auction. (page 1)

Promotion – Developing one or more cards into winners by driving out any higher-ranking cards held by the opponents. (pages 29, 200)

Raise – Supporting partner's suit by bidding the suit at a higher level. (page 7)

Rebid – A second bid by opener or responder. (page 17)

Redouble – A call that increases the bonuses for making or defeating a contract that has already been doubled. It can be used by responder to show about 10 or more points after the opening bid is doubled. (page 135)

Responder – The partner of the opening bidder. (page 2)

Responder's Double – See Negative Double. (page 124)

Ruff(ing) – Play a trump to a trick when holding no cards in the suit led. Same as trumping. (page 27)

Sacrifice – Deliberately overbidding to a contract that is not expected to make in the hope the penalty will be less than the value of the opponents' potential contract. (page 10)

Short Side – The partnership hand with fewer cards in a specific suit. (page 81)

Simple Overcall – A non-jump overcall; an overcall at the cheapest available level. (page 42)

Singleton – A holding of one card in a suit. (page 45)

Slam – A contract to take twelve or thirteen tricks. (page 9)

Small Slam – A contract to take twelve tricks. (page 20)

Stopper – A holding that is likely to prevent the opponents from immediately taking all the tricks in the suit. (page 123)

Strength – The point count value of a hand. (page 1)

Support – The number of cards held in a suit partner has bid. (page 8)

Sure Trick – A trick which can be taken without giving up the lead to the opponents. (page 8)

Takeout Double – A double that asks partner to bid an unbid suit. (pages 28, 39, 84)

Trick Score – The points scored for contracts bid and made. (page 19)

Trumping – Playing a trump on a trick when void in the suit led. (page 9)

Two Level – The second level on the Bidding Ladder. It represents eight tricks. (page 2)

Unbalanced Hand – A hand with a void, a singleton, or more than one doubleton. (page 58)

Unbid Suit – A suit that has not yet been bid during the auction. (page 31)

Undertrick – Each trick by which declarer's side fails to fulfill the contract. (page 21)

Undoubled – A contract that has not been doubled by the opponents. (page 203)

Valuation (Points) – A method of estimating the value of a hand during the auction, usually a combination of values for high cards and length. (pages 39, 85)

Void – A holding of zero cards in a suit. (page 45)

Vulnerable – In rubber bridge, a partnership that has won a game. In duplicate or Chicago scoring, the vulnerability is assigned to each deal. The bonuses and penalties are greater when a partnership is vulnerable than when it is non-vulnerable. (page 20)

Vulnerability – The status of the deal during a round of bridge which affects the size of the bonuses awarded for making or defeating contracts. Bonuses and penalties are higher when declarer's side is vulnerable. (page 20)

WHERE – The denomination in which the contract should be played. (page 9)

Weak Two-bid – An opening suit bid at the two level, other than 2♣, to show a long suit, typically six cards, with less than the values for an opening bid at the one level. (page 4)

Winner – A card held by one of the players that will win a trick when it is played. (page 29)

BARON BARCLAY
BRIDGE SUPPLY

To order books by Audrey Grant,
contact **Baron Barclay Bridge Supply.**

Quantity discounts are available.
We will be happy to send a copy of our
free catalogs upon request.

Baron Barclay Bridge Supply
3600 Chamberlain Lane, Suite 206
Louisville, KY 40241

U.S. and Canada: 1-800-274-2221
Worldwide: 502-426-0410

www.BaronBarclay.com

AUDREY GRANT'S
BETTER BRIDGE

Audrey Grant's Better Bridge
1-888-266-4447
www.BetterBridge.com